**Putting Skill to Work**

# Putting Skill to Work

## How to Create Good Jobs in Uncertain Times

Nichola Lowe

The MIT Press
Cambridge, Massachusetts
London, England

This book was set in Stone Serif and Stone Sans by Westchester Publishing Services. Printed and bound in the United States of America.

Library of Congress Cataloging-in-Publication Data

Names: Lowe, Nichola, author.

Title: Putting skill to work : how to create good jobs in uncertain times / Nichola Lowe.
Description: Cambridge, Massachusetts : The MIT Press, [2021] | Includes bibliographical references and index.
Identifiers: LCCN 2020015013 | ISBN 9780262045162 (hardcover)
Subjects: LCSH: Employees--Training of--United States. | Employer-supported education--United States. | Skilled labor--United States. | Manpower planning--United States.
Classification: LCC HF5549.5.T7 L646 2021 | DDC 658.3/124--dc23
LC record available at https://lccn.loc.gov/2020015013

10  9  8  7  6  5  4  3  2  1

For my son, Oskar

# Contents

# Acknowledgments

Writing a book—even one that is single-authored—is a community endeavor. Many people have supported this project, inspiring by example, seeding new ideas, encouraging me to push my writing further or knowing when to offer a supportive nod. Three women are closest to this work and were essential partners in earlier research that was further developed and integrated for this project: Mary Donegan, Laura Wolf-Powers, and Julie Stern. As co-authors of earlier papers, they encouraged me to develop the work into something larger and more encompassing. Thank you all for your brilliance, your support, and your camaraderie over the years. Working with you has been such a joy, as is watching your own big and bold projects take root. Jennifer Clark, Pierre Clavel, and John Bryson similarly opened early channels for me to put down some of my ideas in writing, ultimately allowing me to see how those loose threads might eventually come together.

This book could not have been completed without many years of conversation and collaboration with Natasha Iskander, my close friend and my comrade in skills investigation. We both set an ambitious target of writing single-authored books around the same time, knowing they would also help us extend the insights we had gained from our earlier hidden talent collaboration. I have learned much from our work together over the years, especially how to theorize while I write, but equally the power of building a story around the voices of those living and innovating good work. But even more exciting than finishing our respective books at roughly the same time is the recent launch of our newest research adventure together, this time exploring an ever more existential challenge to humanity: climate and work.

Many of the foundational ideas for this book were born twenty years ago when I was a graduate student at MIT. While my dissertation research had very little to do with the topic of workforce skill, the courses I took with MIT faculty in urban studies, economics, and political science laid the conceptual foundations for studying workforce skill and connecting intermediation to broader processes of institution building and change. Paul Osterman helped me recognize both the power of labor market institutions and the need to continually document how and under what conditions those institutions evolve to (re)gain power, even while others are forced to retreat. Michael Piore introduced me to the concepts of interpretation and ambiguity, inspiring much of the book's conceptual framework. From Alice Amsden I learned to value the state, but also to consider the underlying processes of influence and engagement on which the capacity to govern is really based. Frank Levy, now my neighbor and fellow Durham walker, has helped me prepare for counterarguments and caveats. Judith Tendler taught me that writing is power, but to achieve it means editing, over and over and over again. And before all of them, Martin Kenney inspired me to research.

Numerous graduate research assistants and students have contributed to this work over the years, including Austin Amandolia, Peter Cvelich, Allison Forbes, Allan Freyer, Carolyn Fryberger, Marcela Gonzales, Brady Gordon, Jamaal Green, Jessica Pearlman, Hilary Pollan, and Tim Quinn, among others. My former student Cara Isher-Witt has been involved the entire duration, helping with early research and, more recently, acting as my trusted copyeditor and writing cheerleader, ensuring I sharpened the prose, clarified what was less obvious, and tempered my tendency (or, as we like to call it, my superpower) to be typo-blind. Peter Wissoker carried me through the book proposal process and convinced me I had a book. Marc Doussard did the most careful of reviews, helping me see both the weak spots and the powerful messages that needed further amplification. I also thank six anonymous reviewers who offered constructive feedback at various stages of book development. Emily Taber at MIT Press added further editing skills to the mix, ensuring a meaningful and enjoyable book writing experience throughout.

Many other economic development researchers and practitioners, as well as colleagues at the University of North Carolina, have cheered me on over the years and helped me cross the finish line: Greg Schrock, Meenu Tewari, Bill Lester, Noreen McDonald, Maryann Feldman, Jesse White, Ferrel Guillory, Peter Coclanis, John Quinterno, Tom White, Mac McCorkle, Nancey Green Leigh, Liz Reynolds, Helen Lawton Smith, Susan Christopherson, Amy Glasmeier, Ranita Jain, Maureen Conway, Amy Blair, Bill Bullock, John

Balchunas, Erica Staley, Janice Goldman, David Wolfe, Rachel Willis, Joan Fitzgerald, Bjorn Asheim, Bill Rohe, Michele Berger, Mark Katz, Eric Downing, and Todd Owen. I especially thank Emil Malizia and Harvey Goldstein, my economic development mentors during my time at UNC, for their continued support and guidance, as well as the UNC Office of the Provost for generously providing me with a funded leave to focus exclusively on this book. Close friends and neighbors—Sumila, Kristina, Cheri, Tara, Tania, Melinda, Maggie, Cynthia, Marcus, Debbie, Paul, Karen, Nina, Darrel, Cassy, Travis, Robin, Henry, Judy, Sally, Paul, Tristan, Charles—let me share bits of my evolving thinking over good food and drink and provided me with much-needed social sustenance and head-clearing breaks.

Above all, I thank my family for nurturing my mental endurance. My sister and my father anticipated many of the questions that needed to be answered throughout this process—and my mother asked the most, always cheering me on while playing the role of the foil in our ongoing debate around technology and work. James, my ever-patient and ever-engaged husband, shared weekly articles and resources in support of my argument, but also knew when I needed to hear the perspective of an informed contrarian, a skill he learned well from Hendrika and Elizabeth, both at the ready, along with Subir, to help sharpen thinking through good, progressive debate. Charles Umbanhowar, James's father, is not with us now to read the final product, but he was there at the start when I first proposed to write a skill-focused book and helped me realize early on the importance of a clear and unambiguous title. And my son, Oskar—to whom I dedicate this, my first book—helps remind me every single day what can be gained for our family and our society from being part of a learning community that is broad-reaching, inclusive, and diverse.

# 1 Our Skill Problem Today

America has a skill problem. But not because of inadequate educational systems or an unprepared generation of younger-aged workers, as some try to claim. The problem is the widespread failure of American businesses to share responsibility for skill development—that is to say, the unwillingness or inability of many employers to invest sufficient resources, time, and energy into work-based learning and the creation of skill-rewarding career pathways that extend economic opportunity to workers on the lowest rungs of the labor market.

At first glance, this claim might seem overstated. On the whole, American businesses do invest more resources in workforce training than US federal or state agencies, suggesting they more than carry their weight.[1] But a deeper dive into both employer and worker levels reveals a highly uneven pattern of investment that threatens to intensify economic disparity: on average, larger firms are more generous and more consistent with workforce training than are their smaller counterparts.[2] This is not a recent phenomenon. Surveys conducted over several decades, whether administered by academic researchers, public agencies, or business consultants, have repeatedly found that smaller businesses are less inclined to train their workforce. And because of this, smaller firms are also more likely to complain that they suffer from a lower-skilled, less qualified workforce compared to firms that are larger in size.[3]

What makes this training imbalance especially troubling is that smaller businesses make up the vast majority of employer firms in the United States. And their numbers keep rising, as larger firms—whether by choice or as the result of investor pressure[4]—outsource more and more functions to smaller suppliers or subcontractors.[5]

Setting aside the issue of firm size, there are other sources of training inequities in play that disproportionately affect low-wage workers already struggling to make ends meet. Most employers, regardless of size, limit support for skill development to those employees who are already highly educated,[6] a phenomenon that labor scholars describe as the "great training paradox." The result is a bifurcated structure that further concentrates rewards at the top of the occupational hierarchy, with few opportunities for advancement reaching those at the bottom.

What are the economic consequences of this skills imbalance? What can be done to encourage employers—particularly smaller-sized firms—to accept greater responsibility for skill development and broaden those opportunities to include lower-ranked workers? And how can organizations that strive to improve working conditions and extend economic opportunity lend a helping hand?

## Maddie's Story, with Three Alternative Endings

To anchor these questions, let me introduce a young woman from South Carolina whose story of economic hardship is immortalized in a harrowing essay by Adam Davidson, economist and co-creator of the radio program *Planet Money*.[7] Since 2012, I have assigned Davidson's long-form article to students in my graduate seminar Planning for Jobs or an undergraduate variant that examines the changing nature of work in twenty-first-century America.

Davidson offers us a glimpse into the work life of Maddie Parlier, who, at the time *Atlantic Monthly* published Davidson's piece in 2012, was a twenty-two-year-old single mother with only a high school degree. Davidson uses her story to shed light on the "job crisis" facing many low-income Americans trapped in dead-end, low-wage, mundane jobs, which for Maddie involved routine tasks that in the near future could easily be completed by a robot replacement. According to Davidson, Maddie's fate (and that of her low-income brethren) is sealed by a lack of college education—that golden ticket into the middle class that remains out of reach for approximately half of America's working-age population.

Over the years, I have drawn on Maddie's story to motivate an in-class activity, asking my students to work together in small groups to map out a different, better future for Maddie and her daughter. Like Maddie, my students are sharp, scrappy, and inquisitive. I am always impressed by the

thoughtfulness and creativity they put into this hypothetical exercise, working together to devise promising alternatives, sometimes after only ten min-
utes of intensive group dialogue. And the proposals they put forward closely
track a mix of solutions offered by prominent labor scholars and analysts
while also drawing out a deeper set of challenges for Maddie and other low-
wage workers if we, as a nation, fail to fully recognize the complexity of the
problem.

As one might expect of students enrolled at North Carolina's flagship public university, some proposals align closely with Davidson's central tenet—
that Maddie's employment prospects will greatly improve if she quits her
unfulfilling day job manufacturing specialized fuel injectors to instead pursue a college degree. And like Davidson, the students put forward as supporting evidence the experience of Maddie's coworker, Luke—another promising
and ambitious young employee with an associate's degree in applied machining from a nearby community college that not only guarantees a better starting salary but clears the path for occupational mobility by opening up the
option to slot into a higher, more secure position at the firm.

Still, each semester there are also skeptics in my class ready to draw out
the limits of this proposed educational fix, with some students stressing
the financial strain that can accompany individual investment in higher
education. As their questioning implies, the decision to leave the job to
pursue further studies carries heavy consequences: Maddie would forgo her
biweekly paycheck, raising additional financial concerns about how she
will feed herself and her daughter, much less pay for quality child care, rent,
and other household essentials. Though federal education funding and welfare payments could provide some temporary relief, doubts still arise about
Maddie's eventual employment prospects: would a college degree actually
guarantee her good employment and prop open the door to the middle
class? And what about her age (including the added years out of the labor
market), her responsibilities as a single mother, or simply her inability to
relocate or commute long hours—do these and other factors stand in the
way of long-term economic security?

Compounding matters further, class discussions often point to a deeper
problem with this standard supply-side educational approach, one that
gnaws at the edges of contemporary debate over income inequality. Simply proposing Maddie leave this company to pursue higher education,
whether toward a two-year associate's or a four-year bachelor's degree, does

absolutely nothing to improve the quality of an entry-level job at Standard Motor Products. Though further education may confer certain advantages for Maddie and society at large,[8] in isolation it would simply open up her bad job for another economically vulnerable applicant. Much like a high-stakes game of musical chairs, someone will inevitability lose out.

Recognizing this economic predicament, I added parameters to this class exercise a few years back. I now include the critical qualifier that any proposal to improve Maddie's circumstances must introduce improvements to the job itself, that is, change how her job is organized and managed, including how Maddie's contribution as a worker gets recognized, rewarded, and advanced with time.

Still, even with these revised guidelines in place, students come up with a range of alternatives. Some, for example, passionately argue for legislated action at the state or local level to boost Maddie's minimum wage. This suggestion is guided by the credible assumption that this higher wage guarantee would ripple through the low-wage labor market, thus benefiting other undervalued workers besides Maddie. Projections by the Economic Policy Institute, a progressive-leaning think tank, reinforce this point. According to the institute's recent calculations, an increase in the federal minimum wage to $10.10 per hour would benefit upward of 17 million low-wage workers in the United States; an additional 23 million workers would experience a sizable earnings bump if the rate were set at $15 per hour.[9] While these numbers would adjust downward if legislated actions remained limited to the subnational or even substate level, they still demonstrate the wide net that is cast with active labor market policy.

So yes, a minimum wage hike could increase Maddie's earnings potential. But could it also generate better career prospects for Maddie within the firm, allowing her to move up the occupational ladder and, in doing so, gain additional skills and secure higher wages? Certainly—if it is assumed that Maddie's employer would have an added incentive to make adjustments to the work environment as a result of this higher wage bill. Some of my students presume this would occur, as do many scholars and activists calling for increased minimum and living wage standards. Their view is that a higher wage requirement would propel Maddie's employer to introduce productivity-enhancing measures at the company to offset some of that additional labor cost, in turn making better use of Maddie's existing yet underutilized talents.

But is that assumption correct? Could Maddie's employer respond to a higher minimum wage in a less inclusive and supportive manner? Could the employer instead adopt alternative cost-cutting measures that would ultimately cost Maddie her job at the company?

This uncertainty is at the heart of a highly polarized debate over minimum wage legislation now raging throughout this country—one that we also engage in my courses. As an advocate for raising minimum wage standards locally and federally, I admit to being most convinced by recent studies that find little to no job loss from a mandated wage increase, suggesting our economy could easily accommodate a universal raise. Especially compelling is a set of "border" studies that use a quasi-experimental design that pairs neighboring jurisdictions with similar economic and industry characteristics, but with one adopting a higher minimum wage standard.[10] Whether these studies look at jurisdictions that approve a higher universal minimum wage or a less-encompassing, industry-targeted living wage, the results show there is *no* significant or precipitous decline in overall employment, despite claims to the contrary by business leaders and conservative politicians. And follow-up studies find that employers that add new jobs after a higher wage ordinance has gone into effect either pass the increased cost on to their clients or adopt cost-saving measures to offset the mandated wage hike.[11] Raising wages is therefore a promising option that could help improve earnings for low-wage workers.

Still, in light of Maddie's precarious economic position, it is important to recognize that these results are simply averages. While a majority of employers in these studied jurisdictions respond to rising minimum wages by continuing to expand employment, ideally improving jobs in the process, others do not. Adam Davidson's own recounting of an in-depth interview with Maddie's employer suggests this individual would fall squarely within this second camp, so convinced his small manufacturing company would struggle to absorb added labor costs that he is already pondering automation to replace entry-level workers, even as competitors consider a job-preserving option. And he is not alone. Interest in automation is growing, especially within US manufacturing and in some cases driven by the desire to use investment in new technology to lower, not increase, overall workforce head count.[12] In fact, a recent study of the effects of higher minimum wages suggests US manufacturers may be particularly sensitive to higher minimum wages compared to their counterparts in place-bound service industries such as retail and restaurants, which benefit from localized market boundaries, with their nearby competitors also accommodating the wage hike.[13]

Still, even within manufacturing, there remains real choice. Manufacturers can respond to higher wage requirements either by shoring up entry-level jobs through upskilling workers *or,* alternatively, by replacing these workers with technological options. But this choice set also highlights the limits to what a blunt policy instrument such as raising wages can achieve in isolation. Back-up action is needed to augment wage legislation and extend economic opportunities throughout the firm. Even scholars involved in pathbreaking minimum and living wage research recognize that legislated higher wage standards are only a starting place, and that more work is needed to translate those wage gains into quality job opportunities and outcomes. That brings us to the third and final set of recommendations my students propose to support Maddie and her family.

With their gaze firmly locked on decisions and dynamics within the firm, students in this third camp have proposed some combination of work-based change and institutional support to make that happen. Often in the mix are recommendations for job-site mentoring, meaning that front-line workers like Maddie would be paired with company engineers or product designers—including technical experts like her college-educated colleague Luke, who, according to Davidson, currently works in isolation from the entry-level workforce. Cross-functional mentoring offers not only the option to facilitate knowledge and idea sharing but also a channel for strengthening peer advocacy, such that higher-ranked workers could attest to the dependability and quality character of new coworkers and from there, lobby for them to receive additional support and greater job security.

Students have also proposed Maddie's employer provide dedicated time for group problem solving, recognizing that the machines she and other entry-level workers are assigned to often generate substandard parts, thus creating an opening for guided discussion and for supervisors to solicit worker input. To deepen this learning, they pitch some kind of employer-sponsored training—formal on-the-job structures, certainly, but augmented through off-site coursework. This option could easily be supported through a company-backed tuition reimbursement plan or a flexible work schedule that would enable Maddie to build on her foundational knowledge of high school math and science, subjects she enjoyed and excelled at as a student.

Picking up on increased media attention, my fall 2016 cohort advocated for Maddie's employer to create a federally registered apprenticeship program, partnering with a neighboring community college to align on-the-job learning with a technically relevant associate's degree or industry-recognized vocational certificate.

Students pitching these work-based learning opportunities often propose that Maddie earn more as she develops new skills and that she be given the chance to move up an organizational or occupational ladder. Some take the argument a step further, confidently stating that these workplace changes will result in an enduring employee-employer relationship that will simultaneously support higher productivity, process innovation, *and* career advancement—a win-win proposal for Maddie and her employer alike.

Their inspiring calls for change help reinforce a larger point: that extending support for skill development is not just about worker advancement. A better-skilled workforce is also a resource for employers to respond to emergent or unanticipated economic and technological challenges. More than just offering a promising solution to rising income inequality, improvements to Maddie's job extend options for industry innovation and thus create the conditions for broad-reaching economic resilience.

Yet when our class discussions return to the details indelibly inscribed in Davidson's original essay, enthusiasm sometimes wanes as students acknowledge that Maddie's employer could be hard-pressed to implement many of these proposed changes, especially in light of a hypercompetitive auto parts market flooded with low-priced products imported from China. Admittedly, there have been semesters where that day's class session ended with students claiming Adam Davidson is probably correct in assuming social mobility is *only* possible if Maddie and others like her leave their dead-end jobs to pursue a college degree. And reflecting on the injustice of that outcome, they also ponder their own enviable economic circumstances—the opportunities that have been handed to them, and for some, the arbitrariness of good luck.

So, is this a pointless academic exercise with little basis in the real world? Am I naively pushing my students—some with aspirations to one day launch their own businesses and thus employ others—in the wrong direction, ignoring a complex set of insurmountable challenges facing both Maddie and her employer that make it impossible to roll out proposed work-based solutions? Is Davidson simply describing our modern-day economy, in which work itself is less critical for skill development and social mobility, with college education standing firmly in its place? Should we accept as inevitable a labor market defined by projections of growing economic and employment displacement, with innovations in robotics and artificial intelligence expected to deepen job insecurity? Or does this exercise instead suggest that we, as a nation, may be contributing to worsening economic inequality by letting firms off the hook for skill development and by shifting too much of that burden to institutions of higher learning and the students they educate? And if so, what can be done to redress this imbalance?

## My Argument in Summary

Inspired by Maddie and other hard-working yet underpaid individuals like her, this book homes in on the issue of skill and how it connects to a larger recurring debate over income inequality in America. It considers what is at stake for our nation—and for future generations of workers—if we continue to privilege channels for skill development that reside outside the firm at the expense of learning processes that happen at and through work itself. Most important, this book offers a scalable solution for getting more employers to accept greater responsibility for skill development, and with it, to extend economic opportunity to workers on the lowest rungs of the US labor market.

Three concepts anchor my core argument that skill is a problem of employment rather than education; together, they help to map a course for institutional action. The first concept involves situating skill development within a larger job quality framework. By this I mean that skill development is not simply a precursor to accessing good jobs, as is often presumed by those advocating for a more educated workforce. Rather, skill development is *constitutive* of a quality job. Put another way, a good job is one in which workers gain access to learning opportunities and employer-sponsored training that can broaden career prospects, both within the firm and across an associated industry. In this regard, training opportunities are not just a bonus or secondary consideration; they are as integral to job quality as high wages, comprehensive benefits, workplace autonomy, and job satisfaction.

Admittedly, numerous writings before this have placed employer support for skill development on equal footing with family-supporting wages and other income-enhancing benefits.[14] The International Labour Organization, an advocacy arm of the United Nations, has long associated skill development with "decent work," reinforcing interconnections between various attributes of a good job, with work-based training opportunities solidly in the mix. Many scholars have done the same. Given this, why would I write a book that calls for still greater attention to skill development? I do so because while the value of skill has been well established, I believe it is imperative that workforce and labor advocates better leverage the *power of skill* to push more American businesses to improve the quality of jobs they offer to existing and future employees.

To help illustrate this possibility, let me introduce a second critical concept: that skill confers shared value on workers and employers precisely because it lies at the intersection of their respective interests. In other words, skill is not something that workers alone cherish, with employers inclined to dismiss its value or relevance—a tension more commonly associated with worker demands for higher wages or more encompassing employment benefits. Rather, skill is typically perceived in a positive light by *both* workers and employers: both want more of it, and also recognize some intrinsic value to its further development. Workers, for their part, seek out new skills to advance their careers, but also to make their daily work lives more fulfilling and meaningful. On the employer side, skill is widely recognized as essential for enhanced productivity and for advancing product and process innovation. This tight coupling is made explicit by the sheer number of employers that are raising the alarm over industry skill shortages, including those fearing the widespread loss of skill as baby boomers are fast aging out of the workforce.

Still, it is important to acknowledge that while workers and employers might share a positive association with skill, they do not always *interpret* skill in the same way. And there are numerous reasons for why their respective views on skill might differ substantially. We can start with the basic issue of what constitutes skill: does it narrowly describe a technical competency or is it broader-reaching, encompassing less tangible forms of cognition, creativity, or social capacity? Another complication involves the question of who is deemed skilled (and who is not), and related to this, who has the authority—the power—to make that determination. Extending things further are deeper existential questions related to where skill resides: are skills possessed or owned by individual workers or are they integral to the work environment and tightly woven into the social fabric of everyday work?

These considerations bring us to the third and final anchoring concept of this book: that there is inherent *ambiguity* to skill that is born out of different perspectives, experiences, and pressures facing workers and employers.[15] By ambiguity, I mean a deep uncertainty around what skill is, who owns it, and how it gets made that can make it difficult for some to recognize its immediate or future value and thus parse its benefits to workers and employers alike. This uncertainty can arise in the workplace through various avenues. It can reinforce employers' inaction by magnifying their fears that investments in on-the-job training will reward other firms at their own expense, if a newly trained worker accepts a job offer elsewhere. Or ambiguity can mean that coworkers view skill and expertise quite differently, in turn creating workplace friction that can undermine employers' attempts to further extend work-based learning.

Many scholars and workforce practitioners are uncomfortable with this uncertainty, so they seek greater clarity and precision through better skills assessment and measurement. I take a contrasting view and argue that there is power in skill ambiguity: extending that uncertainty can prop open the door for institutional action, in turn allowing workforce advocates to cross the threshold into the firm and move employers through a skills-centered transformation to enhance the work experience of economically vulnerable workers and job seekers.

Varying types of worker-supporting institutions, from labor unions to workforce service providers, can and have used firm interest in skill as an initial opening to intervene at the firm level, first by building on the agreement among workers and employers that skill development is valuable for advancing economic opportunity and progress. Moving beyond the initial consensus, these institutions then strengthen their worker advocacy role by harnessing (and sometimes heightening) uncertainty around skill. They can engage skill ambiguity to advance broader conceptions of expertise, in this way advocating for lower-ranked workers who might otherwise be cursorily dismissed by their employers or coworkers as unskilled or underqualified. By engaging with uncertainty they can push revisionist thinking, leading employers through a renegotiation over what is meant by skill and who should contribute to its development and share its many benefits.[16] And they can redirect some of that uncertainty to help employers get unstuck, pushing them to reinterpret skill investment as critical to future business success rather than as an immediate liability or risk—in other words, strengthening the business case for building enduring twenty-first-century training systems within the firm that can outlast the comings and goings of any single individual.

Once these workforce advocates have shifted employer thinking and action around skill, they are well positioned to promote other improvements to job quality, becoming even stronger advocates for the workers whose skills they have helped elucidate, defend, and promote. They can then extend negotiations around skill to influence thornier aspects of employment relations that involve greater worker-employer tension, such as negotiations over higher wages and more extensive worker benefits (figure 1.1). Equally, they can link employer investments in workforce skill to critical choices in technology adoption, guiding employers to implement new and improved technologies in ways that enhance job quality and grow the business in ways that expand rather than cut overall jobs. And building from there, these workforce advocates can push employers to reevaluate their strategies for innovation and realize even greater gains for the business—and thus their associated industries—when improved processes and products are *inclusive* of workers across the entire organizational and educational spectrum. In this regard, uncertainty around skill is not a problem to be hastily fixed or resolved; it is a bonding material and thus a powerful resource that institutional actors can use to keep the interests of workers and employers in closer alignment.

### Mediating Skill

So who are the workforce advocates that recognize this power in skill? This book focuses on workforce institutions that adopt a "dual-customer" approach, serving both job seekers and employers, in order to enhance employment prospects through organizational or industry expansion.[17] These institutions are commonly referred to as a *workforce intermediaries* and

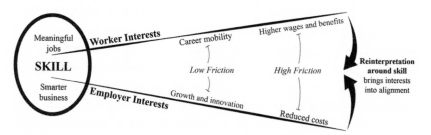

**Figure 1.1**
Reinterpretation around skill ambiguity benefits workers and employers.

are diverse in their institutional origins and affiliations: some are the out-growth of community-based nonprofit organizations, others are extensions of well-established labor unions, and still others are branches of a county- or state-funded community college system. The ones I feature all employ strategies that help firms deepen their commitment to skill development by formalizing internal structures for recognizing and rewarding work-based learning and occupational mobility. Throughout this book, I refer to these as strategies of *skill reinterpretation*.

Admittedly, as part of this strategic approach, workforce intermediaries also link employer firms—and by extension their front-line workers—to educational institutions, especially community and vocational colleges, that offer customized training and technical assistance to firms, along with portable credentials for workers. But this institutional partnering represents much more than the typical supply-side push for job seekers to rack up more credentials or degrees; workforce intermediaries tap these educational partners as a means to strengthen their influence over employers and to construct an external scaffolding from which to build and reinforce skill development opportunities and supports within firms.

In partnering with educational institutions to utilize existing course offer-ings and sources of industry and training expertise, these intermediaries help reduce employer training costs. But they also make use of external training services so that firms' internal resources can be reallocated to increased sup-port of employees' career development through work-based learning. The result is a model that forges *interdependencies* between employers and educa-tional institutions in order to create greater capacity to support skill develop-ment. What ultimately emerges is an integrated institutional platform that recognizes and reinforces skill development as a shared social commitment and responsibility.

It is estimated that there are now around 1,000 workforce intermediar-ies in the United States, more if we include new programs and initiatives embedded within publicly funded community colleges. The ones that fea-ture most prominently in this book represent a subset called sector-based intermediaries; they specialize in a particular sector or industry and usu-ally limit that industry involvement to a specific locality, city, or (substate) region. My focus is on sector-based intermediaries that support manufactur-ing firms and their workers, helping develop, or in some cases reestablish, skill-centered pathways for occupational advancement. These sector-based intermediaries benefit from deep knowledge of the manufacturing industries they target. This means that not only are they able to adjust their strategies of reinterpretation to address industry-specific workforce challenges, they are also able to leverage other industry experts to bring in additional technical and business supports to complement skill-related changes.

As is common in workforce intermediation, the institutional actors featured in this book mostly target their efforts toward small and medium-sized manufacturing employer firms, recognizing that these firms often face greater resource and management constraints relative to their larger-sized counterparts. Additionally, these intermediaries have their eye on low-paying frontline manufacturing jobs and the workers that occupy them, and thus strive to extend opportunities for skill development down to the lowest level of the organization. In other words, their work moves down the career ladder to reach entry-level manufacturing workers like Maddie Parlier.

But why focus on US manufacturing, which has long created quality job opportunities for workers with limited formal education beyond a high school degree? Why not instead shift the emphasis to low-wage services, which employ significantly larger numbers of low-wage, less educated workers? Because access to high-quality, well-paying jobs in manufacturing is no longer guaranteed. In recent decades, the wage premium historically associated with jobs in US manufacturing has shrunk considerably—and long-term job security is equally threatened as more and more American-based manufacturing firms turn to lower-paying staffing agencies to manage employment growth.[18] While it is true that well-paying jobs in manufacturing can still be had, it is also the case that these jobs are now much harder to secure for less educated workers than in previous decades—and this suggests a need for focused institutional intervention.

Some of this decline in quality manufacturing employment is attributable to the weakening influence of labor unions—meaning the loss of a critical institutional gatekeeper that long held manufacturing companies accountable to broad-reaching job quality standards, including high wages, good benefits, and career pathways.[19] But union decline is itself reflective of overall manufacturing job loss, which has intensified in recent decades, with American manufacturers shedding close to a quarter of all jobs (six million in total) from 2000 to 2010. Economists now attribute much of this employment volatility to global economic integration and increased competition from lower-cost manufacturing nations such as China.[20] As mentioned earlier, Maddie's own employer, Standard Motor, is facing this global competitive challenge, which suggests that it is not just front-line manufacturing workers that are struggling: employers too face mounting pressure from international competitors, which curtails their ability to generate and sustain quality employment.

Yet even with these entangled threats of global competition and labor union decline, there is compelling evidence that American manufacturing firms can regain some ground, adding more and better jobs in the future.[21] Research by the economist Susan Houseman suggests as much by identifying a wide array of product-making industries in the United States with historically low productivity rates.[22] Once computer and electronics manufacturing is removed from the analysis, Houseman finds US manufacturing productivity has actually underperformed relative to all other private sector industries. And this weak performance speaks not only to an unrealized growth potential but also to the possibility for targeted institutional support to guide American manufacturing development and expansion going forward.

Of course, with global competition a major factor in manufacturing job loss, one option is simply to enact stronger trade protections—a policy choice favored by the Trump administration, which has responded to manufacturing job decline by arbitrarily increasing tariffs and inciting a trade war with China and other critical trade partners. But this is not the only option. An alternative to this narrowly defensive tactic is coordinated institutional action to proactively enhance industry performance and better position American-based firms to become more globally competitive.[23] Arguments in favor of more comprehensive industrial policy often draw inspiration from European and Asian nations that have seen steady gains in manufacturing employment as a result of sustained and coordinated public investments in innovation, technical assistance, and workforce development. Manufacturing industries in these nations also face some threat from lower-wage countries, but well-rounded policy supports ensure that manufacturing firms can respond in ways that benefit, rather than harm, their own production workforce.

In the United States, several existing institutional levers exist that, with further government support, could scale up to a similarly robust policy platform—including ever-popular federal initiatives such as the Manufacturing Extension Partnership and Manufacturing USA Institutes. But even if the United States commits to a more aggressive national policy framework in support of manufacturing growth, the question remains: Who will have access to the new and improved manufacturing jobs that this policy stance aims to create? The current labor market uncertainty speaks to the need for policy leaders to expand the institutional lens further in support of manufacturing workers, not just the businesses that employ them. That is to say, there is a need to marshal institutional and policy resources to advance both industrial performance and economic opportunity, a challenge for which strategies of skill reinterpretation are particularly well suited.

## Expanding Intermediation

This book is certainly not the first to recognize the ongoing contribution of sector-focused workforce intermediaries to enhancing the economic standing of low-income workers. While workforce intermediaries have long existed in the United States, their visibility increased in the early 1990s with a high-profile convening of progressive foundations, labor scholars, and practitioners. Since then, concurrent and complementary efforts have been undertaken to expand the number of workforce intermediaries in the United States, aided by generous funding commitments and support from philanthropic foundations and alliances such as the Annie E. Casey Foundation, the Ford Foundation, and the National Fund for Workforce Solutions, as well as through such practitioner preparation programs as the Aspen Institute's Sector Skills Academy. A rich and detailed body of writings exists on workforce intermediation, not only providing illustrative and inspiring examples through in-depth case studies but also demonstrating employment and wage gains through rigorous experimental and quasi-experimental analysis.[24]

In their idealized form, workforce intermediaries would be well positioned to intervene to increase economic opportunities for low-income workers and job seekers by influencing employer decision-making with respect to hiring, wage-setting, and advancement. In reality, however, many practitioners within these intermediaries acknowledge the difficulties of persuading employers to make changes to existing organizational structures. This has led some intermediaries to simply double down on their provision of social services, including pre-employment training, offering a bundle of supports to low-income individuals, and putting in place a safety net should their attempts to secure well-paying jobs fail.[25] And while these intermediaries certainty direct job seekers to "high-road" employers that already provide quality jobs, they often struggle to take their work a step further to effectively transform "bad jobs into good."

Another challenge facing workforce intermediaries is mission creep. With workforce intermediaries filling a critical labor market void left in the wake of labor union decline, there is added pressure to get involved in national and regional labor campaigns in support of worker rights, living wages, and better working conditions.[26] But the time spent on organizing could push employer engagement more to the sidelines and thus come at the expense of the core mission: building institutional power by influencing employers' decisions in the workplace.

This book draws attention to strategies that are often the hardest for intermediaries to support and sustain: employer engagement. Garnering insights from intermediaries that have successfully used strategies of employer engagement to make headway with manufacturing businesses, I see my goal as one of motivating continued progress—and to do so by also highlighting enabling resources and supports, including strategic partnerships, that can help intermediaries strengthen their industry influence and institutional reach.

With that in mind, this book explores the actions of several well-established and well-documented workforce intermediaries. But it telescopes out too. Studies of workforce intermediation (and economic development more generally) have long praised the experimental nature of nongovernmental organizations, which often have greater leeway to tinker and tweak strategies as they are not limited to the formal structures or bounds of public agencies. Still, there is near consensus that further expansion of workforce intermediation requires strong involvement by public institutions, not just as distant or secondary partners in intermediation but as central drivers and coordinating entities that can bring to the table new resources, business networks, and policymaking capacity.

To that end, I also consider the contributions of more recent initiatives that enact similar strategies within well-resourced public educational systems. At one level, these particular cases reveal additional capacity for government-funded institutions to become more like their nonprofit workforce counterparts, leveraging existing educational and training resources to gain greater influence over employer decisions. They suggest that there is ample opportunity for public community colleges, school districts, and state-funded vocational training centers to do more to respond to industry calls for a more skilled workforce: they too can advance job quality standards by elevating the expectation that employers share more responsibility for skill development and build their internal training capacity to ensure that is possible. But more than this, these cases also point to strategies that workforce systems can use to weather economic downturns and navigate political roadblocks, in turn offering transferable lessons that could benefit intermediaries of all types.

## The Chapters Ahead

Skill is a recurring topic in the national debate over rising income inequality, and the differing perspectives on this issue offer a useful starting place for situating strategies of skill reinterpretation. Chapter 2 begins by outlining the broad terms of that debate, which intensified in the wake of the Great Recession and undergirds calls for educational institutions to better address industry skill needs. Critics have rightly questioned blanket claims of industry skill shortages, some putting forward the compelling counterargument that firms exacerbate their own shortages by failing to pay sufficiently high wages. But, I argue, repeated claims by employers of skill shortages should not be dismissed outright. Rather, they provide an opening for alternative labor market interventions—not designed to serve employers the skills they claim to need but rather to shift how employers interpret skill and to explicate their social responsibility for its development.

The chapter then makes room for these interventions by relaxing the standard assumption that skill is a fixed, measurable, easily defined concept. I draw inspiration from ethnographic studies of work to present skill as a socially constructed resource, one that is also ambiguous, fluid, and open to contestation. This reframing helps relieve some of the pressure on workforce practitioners to definitively measure the precise skill needs of employers and industries and allows them instead to focus on negotiations with employers, deepening their interventions to shape and reshape employers' understanding of skill and its enduring value. It also allows us to recognize formative efforts by labor unions to contest employer attempts to appropriate, control, or undervalue workforce skill, with unions pushing to establish protective structures that would guarantee workers access to extensive on-the-job training and tether those supports to skill-rewarding wages and industry-recognized portable credentials.

Chapters 3 through 5 are the empirical heart of this book, situating strategies of skill reinterpretation in a contemporary economic and political landscape mindful of challenges and opportunities for worker advocacy and employer engagement. The precipitous decline of unions in the United States does not mean the end to negotiations around skill. Rather, other worker advocates have stepped into this institutional void, bringing new strategies and resources to the table. Drawing on in-depth interviews with workforce practitioners, educators, business owners in US manufacturing, and their workers, I describe how workforce intermediaries are helping employers support occupational mobility by extending opportunities for skill development to less educated workers and job seekers. I also highlight emerging challenges that threaten the ability of these mediating workforce institutions to sustain and scale up interventions without further political and policy support.

Chapter 3 unpacks the concept of sectoral workforce intermediation in relation to skill. Numerous workforce intermediaries in the United States originated in response to manufacturing employers' perception of a skill shortage in their respective regional economy. But not all intermediaries have been able to engage employers in a negotiated process around skill. This chapter features several examples of success, presenting a composite picture of manufacturing-focused intermediaries in Chicago, Cincinnati, Cleveland, Milwaukee, and Pittsburgh to better understand how they successfully apply strategies of skill reinterpretation to advance opportunities for individuals who lack college degrees. It also explores how these same intermediaries work with small and medium-sized manufacturers, including by partnering with technical assistance providers to transform investments in worker training into overall gains in productivity and innovative capacity.

Chapter 4 digs deeper into a Chicago-based workforce intermediary to examine how these same strategies have been applied to help Black high school students transition into manufacturing careers by helping smaller-sized manufacturing firms diversify their workforce. This more encompassing approach not only helps align training protocols across the entire manufacturing workforce, it also reduces racial and intergenerational conflict at the worksite. This chapter also illustrates both the gains and stresses when workforce intermediaries partner with educational institutions, including public school systems, to reinforce skill development practices and improvements internal to firms. The nonprofit intermediary at the core of this chapter is at the mercy of a large educational bureaucracy. The case speaks to its institutional vulnerability, but equally points to further opportunities for institutional scaling up both within and outside the boundaries of public education systems.

In chapter 5, I feature workforce intermediaries that are helping larger, well-resourced manufacturers strengthen their existing internal training programs by externalizing more standard training protocols through the creation of industry-recognized community college certificate courses. While this effort is less focused on effecting change within firms, the workforce systems that are being created nonetheless have that residual effect, and the capacity to influence even more organizational change going forward. To illustrate this development, I focus on a network of pioneering community colleges in North Carolina that coordinates training support for biopharmaceutical manufacturers. Colleges in this network adapt employee training and placement services to open paths into high-growth firms for less educated job seekers. With its recent expansion to food, beverage, and natural product manufacturing, this community college network has strengthened the institutional base for influencing employer investments in and improvements to firm-specific training and mentoring.

## Target Audience

The central role of skill in the national discourse on expanding economic opportunity makes the book extremely timely. I have written the empirical chapters with the goal of giving them broad interdisciplinary appeal for scholars of human resource management, labor history, education policy, social work, and economic development. But an equally important audience for me is economic and workforce development practitioners, including program evaluators and policy analysts. While chapter 2 largely engages ongoing academic debates, including the highly influential economic theory of skills-biased technical change, I connect that technical discussion to current public and policy debates over income inequality, education, technological change, and job quality. I do this not only to illustrate the influence of established economic theories on mainstream policy and public discourse but also to drive home the message that we need a more nuanced interpretative framework for transforming theory into institutional action.

For practitioners who are well entrenched in the tight-knit world of workforce intermediation, many of the strategies and recommendations will sound familiar; they reflect, in part, the thoughtful insights that workforce practitioners have shared in their reports and analytical writings over the years. With this book, I hope to add to the existing body of work, providing findings from new empirical research while also helping to bring existing insights to a wider audience.

Policymakers today are eager to take meaningful action to address America's stark and growing economic polarization. They are searching for real solutions to improve job quality—and in this process, they frequently reference the need for skill development. By bringing the skill-focused efforts of workplace intermediaries to the forefront of the discussion, I hope to inspire more decision-makers to build on what practitioners already know works well in this institutional space. In making the case for reinterpreting skill—and stressing the point that skill is frequently misunderstood, and therein lies its transformative power—my ultimate goal is to encourage more intermediaries to deepen their strategies of employer engagement and more forcefully advocate that firms foster economic opportunity by committing to workplace improvements.

### Skilled with Technology

This book comes at a time of heightened American political anxiety and its serious consequences for already vulnerable workers. Despite claims of supporting the "common (working) man," the Trump administration swiftly reversed crucial Obama-era actions that helped advance worker rights and protections, and more threats to labor legislation and related social supports loom on the horizon.[27] Labor advocacy is thus at a critical juncture. Yes, signs are promising that the "Fight for $15" and related living wage campaigns will continue to advance at the subnational level despite this federal reversal, with progressive political leaders ready to double down on local labor standards. Still, efforts to raise the wage floor, while necessary, are insufficient for fully addressing economic vulnerability; doing so must also involve improved job quality commitments and career mobility opportunities. Worker rights advocates also need to find ways to directly engage US employers and to connect demands for higher wages and better working conditions to strategies that influence business practice from the inside out.

Sector initiatives, like those described in this book, provide a promising institutional platform from which to engage employers and influence thinking and decision-making around skill development and recognition, all the way to the shop floor. But more can be done to extend this intermediary model and widen its labor market impact and reach.

There are numerous options for skill-focused workforce intermediation to expand beyond the industries and regions described in this book. Promoting similar strategies in low-wage service industries, for example, could benefit a wide swath of the national workforce, as jobs in health care, customer service, and retail are projected to generate high levels of future job growth—a move that the Aspen Institute, a long-standing supporter of workforce intermediaries, is helping to advance through a recent initiative called Reimagining Retail. But it is not just think tanks and nonprofits that have a role to play. State and local government agencies can also extend the labor market reach of workforce intermediaries. Even with lackluster workforce support from the federal government, local jurisdictions can leverage the 2014 Federal Workforce Opportunity and Innovation Act, which mandates that state governments use sector approaches for allocating federal funds in support of workforce development. Growing bipartisan support for apprenticeship and related work-based learning programs also opens the door for coordinated institutional action. Federally registered apprenticeship programs require more on-the-job training than classroom learning, meaning there is a built-in institutional mechanism for requiring sponsoring employers to share greater responsibility for skill development. Even if future growth in registered apprenticeships lags expectations, the increasing popularity of the apprenticeship concept among American business leaders could prove useful for advancing other models of work-based learning. Furthermore, a vast network of national and regional philanthropic foundations exists to help public agencies expand workforce intermediation through supplemental funding and technical assistance. By connecting these various threads, workforce advocates have the power to influence dynamics of work by ensuring skill development opportunities are broad-reaching and high impact.

But can intermediation around skill have an even more profound economic and political impact? I explore this question in the sixth and final chapter, proposing additional steps for moving strategies of skill reinterpretation into mainstream economic development. In other words, rather than containing workforce intermediaries within a narrow description of their workforce contributions, I lay out a path for connecting these same actors and their skill-focused strategies to a broader institutional goal of industry innovation and technological progress.

There is already an intimate and complicated relationship between skill and technological change that workforce intermediaries can leverage. Many analysts, past and present, make explicit reference to the dynamic interaction between technology and skill when reflecting on protracted periods of economic insecurity. For now, the dominant view is that technological change will render certain skill sets worthless and obsolete. To resolve this disconnect, the most commonly proposed solution is also that suggested by Adam Davidson for Maddie in 2012: workers facing imminent threat of skills obsolescence should enroll in formal educational programs that promise to resolve this technology-induced skills mismatch. In this "skills mismatch" framing, institutions are expected to step in once firms have chosen new technologies and implementation is well under way; the assumption among employers is that these institutions will be on call, prepared to update and refine workforce skills in response to industry's adoption of new technology.

But as I argue in chapter 6, the relationship between skill and technology can play out quite differently, and with far-reaching implications for entry-level and front-line workers. An alternative approach is already in the works and yielding promising results on which to build. It involves mediated institutional actions that position workforce skill as critical to technological decision-making from the start, not as an afterthought or a follow-on reaction. With this intermediation, employers learn there is value to having front-line workers continually participate in technology decisions and development. And by extension, proposed technological changes are also subject to focused advocacy, especially in support of workers whose skill sets might, on the surface, seem tangential to innovation. Advocates can challenge this myopic perspective on worker equity grounds but also help employers realize worker exclusion is potentially self-defeatist and detrimental to future business success.

This alternative vision does not treat technological advancement as predetermined and inevitable. Nor does it relegate workforce institutions to the back seat. Rather, it entails the formation of new institutional connections and alliances to rebalance the *politics of skill*,[28] with renewed political focus not just on strengthening worker negotiations in the workplace but also on anchoring those gains to a broader, shared vision of *inclusive innovation*. In this unfolding future, power is not held by technology (or technologists) but lies in how institutional agents help technology designers, developers, and users—including employers—engage front-line workers in processes of innovation, including a reinterpretation of technological choices. In this context, it is no longer enough to say, with Shoshana Zuboff, that "new choices are laid open by [new] technologies."[29] What is most critical is an open and shared process of discovery, with front-line workers more centrally involved in shaping novel technologies and new technological applications.

As I also illustrate in the concluding chapter, this intersection of inclusion and innovation offers an opportunity for new forms of labor advocacy to arise that treat skill development and innovation as two sides of the same coin. As labor advocates forge these new institutional partnerships, they must reconcile older labor traditions, which focused on strengthening skill through improved labor processes internal to a firm, with more recent social and labor movements that seek to build worker mobilization and political power.[30] But equally, they need to push back against the ever-popular assumption—one too happily advanced by technology futurists, influencers, and financiers in Silicon Valley and other high-tech hubs—that industry innovation entails technological changes that are inherently disruptive to jobs and damaging for the less educated workers that hold them.[31] More than a critique of technological hubris, we need this counter-response to include coordinated strategies that empower workforce institutions to elevate their influence over technology development and choice, and not just step in ex post facto with skills to match the latest technological imperative, paradigm, or fad. As this book demonstrates, strategies of skill reinterpretation can be amended to support the work of the future, promoting workers' skills as crucial to technological progress by also reestablishing skill development as a revered and protected worker right.

## 2 (Re)Placing Skill in the Workplace

Adam Davidson is not alone in expressing genuine, heartfelt concern over the growing economic vulnerability of less educated workers and job seekers in the United States today. In recent decades, labor economists have turned their attention to the fate of workers like Maddie—individuals, young and old, with little to no formal education beyond a high school degree or GED and with demanding family obligations, be they financial support or care of a family member, that make it difficult if not impossible to uproot and move in search of better employment prospects. But economists also disagree over how best to extend opportunities for upward mobility to less educated individuals, and they disagree more generally over what kind of institutional interventions are needed to increase the likelihood that low-wage workers like Maddie will advance to well-paying, good-quality jobs. It is in the details of this evolving policy debate—one that ultimately spills over into other social science disciplines and professions—that we find room for novel yet scalable forms of coordinated institutional action to enhance the capacity of US employers to better support their workforce.

At the core of this debate is growing national concern over income inequality. In recent decades income inequality has risen to levels no longer considered within acceptable bounds by most mainstream economists; nor has such a surge in inequality been limited to a few volatile years within a much larger period of broadly shared prosperity. Recent estimates by the Organisation for Economic Co-operation and Development (OECD) and other reputable international organizations find the United States is now the *most* inequitable advanced industrial economy in the world; the United Kingdom, with its similar liberal market regime, is a very close second.[1]

Rising inequality in America is not simply attributable to faster rates of income growth among high earners, with incomes for all others continuing to rise steadily, if at a slightly slower rate. No: the income gap in the United States is expansive, growing, and drawn out. It reflects exponential growth at the top of the national income bracket over a period of four decades during which real wages at the middle and bottom have stagnated or, for many, declined.[2] In other words, this is not a "rising tide" scenario, with all income groups enjoying a larger slice of an ever-expanding economic pie, though with lower income brackets receiving a slightly smaller portion. Rather, there is clear evidence of upward redistribution and historic levels of income concentration benefiting those firmly stationed at the top, with the vast majority of others experiencing income stagnation or loss.[3]

What is contributing to rising income inequality in the United States? And how does skill development, the focus of this book, relate to inequality?

With each subsequent economic downturn—including the Great Recession of 2008–2009—debate heats up over the relationship between inequality and skill. For those on one side of this debate, the focus is almost exclusively on the polarizing effects of skill-displacing technologies. They argue that technological advances contribute to rising income inequality because those advances, if widely adopted, drastically alter which skill sets and related occupational specializations remain valuable and thus well remunerated. We see this idea playing out in the wake of the Great Recession, captured in the near daily publication of alarmist editorials and policy briefs that predict widespread job loss or displacement from automation, including recent applications in artificial intelligence and machine learning that support a transition to driverless or autonomous vehicles. But the assumption that technological advances will render certain skill sets obsolete is nothing new—in fact, it is a familiar prognostication that resurfaces time and time again, dating back several decades, if not centuries.

Academic versions of this argument gained prominence in the late 1980s as signs of growing wage disparities emerged between groups of manufacturing workers.[4] Economists attributed this uneven wage pattern to increasing employer demand for skilled manufacturing workers in the 1980s and early 1990s, with "skilled" workers classified not just as having more years of manufacturing experience but also as entering the labor market with higher levels of formal education. Drawing inspiration from earlier work on the complementary relationship between workforce skill and technological progress,[5] economists constructed an empirically testable theory they called "skill-biased technical change," which they anchored to a seemingly straightforward argument that individuals lacking requisite knowledge of emerging technologies would experience slower rates of wage growth relative to those with greater experience and mastery in this area.[6] For economists writing in the 1980s, the relevant technological change in question was computerized microprocessing,[7] with additional analysis indicating that it was the routinized nature of certain tasks that increased the risk that wages—and thus workers assigned those tasks—would be negatively affected by the adoption of computerized technologies.[8] In line with neoclassical economics, the effects of technological change on wage disparity would presumably be magnified through established laws of supply and demand, the assumption being that a combination of higher demand for expertise in microprocessing and an initially constrained supply of individuals possessing those highly sought-after skills would drive up wages offered for computer-savvy workers compared to their less skilled counterparts.[9] By this same logic, further advances in technology should increase (or replenish) the supply of unskilled workers at the bottom of the labor pool and thus maintain, even deepen, the widening wage gap.

In summary, the theory of skill-biased technical change assumes that intensified levels of income inequality reflect a technologically-induced *skills mismatch*, with a rising number of workers facing wage stagnation or relative wage decline because they lack the requisite skill sets demanded by US businesses and employers. In other words, their lack of in-demand skills—but little else—explains why they are trapped at the bottom of the earnings scale.

This "skills mismatch" explanation continues to inform contemporary writings on income inequality.[10] Widely bandied-about terms such as "structural unemployment," "technological unemployment," and the "new normal" are shorthand expressions of this same argument and reflect continuing concern about the displacing effects of modern-day automation and technologically induced restructuring on certain jobs and workers.[11] And economic predictions of widespread job loss are no longer solely focused on workers trapped in low-wage jobs: there is growing concern that middle-income jobs will soon hollow out, with manufacturing occupations once presumed immune to technological change facing the greatest risk of long-term, permanent displacement[12]—a troubling phenomenon that economists have termed labor market polarization.[13]

Because the skills mismatch explanation associates shifting skill demands with new technological applications, its proponents often recommend solutions in line with Adam Davidson's recommendation for Maddie Parlier and other low-wage workers like her: attaining a higher level of formal education.[14] The assumption is that investing in higher education will not just buffer job seekers from the displacing effects of present-day technological change but will also enable them to stay abreast of continuous changes in skill demand. Education will give them the necessary tools and capabilities— namely, critical thinking skills and an aptitude for additional training—to adjust to further "structural" changes when innovations in technology once again disrupt career trajectories and reorient employment prospects.

Admittedly, discussions of how best to advance an educational solution have evolved in recent decades and now include the ever-important question of how to also make higher education more accessible and affordable.[15] Leading up to the 2008–2009 Great Recession, economists placed much of the policy emphasis on more people attaining university degrees, especially bachelor's degrees. In recent years, however, both economists and social scientists have broadened the list of desirable credentials to include associate's degrees, technical certificates, and other industry-recognized credentials.[16] Even with these new options added to the educational menu, however, the core logic remains the same: increased educational attainment is necessary for US workers to stay in step with new technologies and the resulting skill requirements. Without this, workers will be consigned to low-wage, poor-quality jobs.

## The Institutional Turn

Of course, few critics would challenge proposals to extend educational opportunities to workers within the United States, especially if those interventions were designed to reduce financial hardship and make it easier for lower-income individuals to secure a high-quality education. There are as well numerous reinforcing benefits at the individual and societal level when barriers to higher education and degree completion are removed. Still, what many labor scholars find problematic with this "skill-biased" theory is its blindness to other moderating factors that contribute to inequality irrespective of technological change. In their view—one I share—rising income inequality is not an inevitable by-product of a sudden (or sustained) exogenous technological change or "shock." It stems from a less visible, disquieting confluence of institutional factors that range from stalled progress in raising the federal minimum wage to intentional strategies of employers and policymakers to weakened labor union power and the removal of other forms of labor protection.[17]

Early institutionalists focused their critique on the purported association between growing wage gaps and the diffusion of microprocessing. Drawing on disaggregated industry and occupational data, a series of published accounts from the 1990s and early 2000s revealed widespread evidence of wage stagnation, even among computer-heavy industries that experienced a significant upswing in educational attainment among workers.[18] In other words, even workers that had acquired highly sought-after technical skills were not experiencing the enviable wage bump that skill-biased models had anticipated. And this disconnect between wage gains and desired skill continues to play out today. Recent research by Nancy Folbre and Richard Freeman has found strong evidence of widely varying earnings among US workers with near-equivalent skill sets, reinforcing the point that three decades of rising income inequality in the United States have little connection to technology-shifting requirements.[19]

But linking rising inequality to a slow-moving, insidious institutional transformation requires more than quantitative analysis of the trajectory of technological change. Historical and contextual detail is needed to capture this institutional shift and trace its downward effect on wages and working conditions. Institutional accounts often pin the start of this structural labor market shift on Ronald Reagan's infamous decision to battle it out with the Professional Air Traffic Controllers Organization (PATCO) union and replace striking air traffic controllers in the name of national security. This action, in combination with pro-business interventions around that time, signaled a significant shift in federal policy and opened the possibility for state governments to overtly challenge unions and other labor protections.[20] The resulting process of institutional decay has played out over several decades and at multiple, reinforcing scales, with sustained effects that continue to restrict economic opportunity for low- and middle-income American workers today.[21]

How does skill fit within this institutionalist framework? Like those on the skill-biased side of this debate, institutionalist labor scholars writing about income and wage inequality in the 1990s and the first half of the 2000s made room in their analyses for workforce skill. But they placed skill—and in particular, processes of skill formation—within a more nuanced and institutionally encompassing framework that linked the institutional restructuring of the labor market to declining opportunities for skill-based occupational mobility. Inspired by the seminal writings of Peter B. Doeringer and Michael J. Piore,[22] institutionalist accounts written through the early 2000s looked for explanations beyond declining union power or shifting regulatory orientation; while these were essential factors within the overall institutional narrative, they were not the only institutional source of economic inequity.

Institutionalists in this period also looked *within* firms, pointing to a concurrent unraveling of *internal labor markets* that American employers had previously supported in the post–World War II period. The turning point was around 1980. Up until then, most American-based firms extended on-the-job training to workers at all occupational levels, with robust internal practices and structures in place to protect and reward workers for this skill-enhanced learning. This is not to say all firms supported training at equally generous and sophisticated levels. But even with varying levels of investment, the general convention was for employer-supported training to reach far down the occupational ladder, benefiting especially entry-level and front-line workers with skill development opportunities.

While there is some disagreement over the immediate causes of this institutional turn in the early 1980s—some scholars argue it was reflective of a major ideological break in corporate values, while others point instead to complications from global trade that forced employers to tighten their belts—its effect on workforce practices is unambiguous. Institutional accounts capture in great detail the reduced commitment by US employers to workforce training and the chilling effect on job quality that came from disrupting skill-enhancing structures long associated with occupational mobility and advancement within the American workplace.[23]

As a result of institutional scholars' focus on skill, we can say with great confidence that rising inequality throughout the 1980s and 1990s was not simply the result of institutional shifts outside the firm, such as the unraveling of federal labor protections, or the failure of governing officials to enact higher minimum wage guarantees, or even the precipitous drop in union representation, though all of these were in play. Equally problematic was the diminished willingness (or capacity) of American employers to maintain support for employee training and related career-enhancing pathways, including mobility opportunities to allow entry-level workers to progress through years of service and accumulated work experience into influential management roles.[24] The journalist Rick Wartzman aptly characterizes this notable reversal in business and corporate strategy in his book *The End of Loyalty* as representing a breakdown in the post–World War II social contract between American employer and employee.[25] In tearing up this contract, employers ultimately reneged on their commitments to broad-reaching workforce development, replacing once inclusive training systems with incomplete internal supports that touched fewer and fewer workers and also established an impenetrable divide between elite management roles and the front-line workforce.[26]

Institutionalist explanations for rising income inequality gained traction in the second half of the 1990s and early 2000s by conceptually aligning with research, analysis, and advocacy coming out of sociology, urban planning, and labor history.[27] To build stronger evidence in support of this alternative explanation to the dominant skill-biased perspective, institutional labor economists frequently crossed disciplinary and methodological boundaries and drew on a mix of innovative data sources, both qualitative and quantitative.[28] Labor scholars and economists in this camp also positioned themselves as trusted advisers to labor unions and other labor market intermediaries, helping inform efforts to protect or rebuild internal labor market structures.[29]

But equally important, by considering the internal workings of firms—not just their external institutional reinforcements—institutional scholars also forged strong analytical connections to organizational theory and business strategy.[30] Whereas studies of skill-biased technical change tended to limit their analysis to aggregate national or regional economic data, institutional research included in-depth case studies and case comparisons involving specific firms and organizational settings in order to draw a more complete institutional picture. Extending from this, institutional scholars also established industry expertise, in the process gaining a deeper appreciation for how industry-specific dynamics reflected and produced different kinds of work-enhancing institutional structures and supports.[31]

In summary, institutionalists writing in the run-up to the twenty-first century offered a compelling alternative explanation for income inequality to the dominant technology-centric narrative at the time. Their gaze was trained on external institutional structures for sure—most notably the weakening of labor union influence and the reversal of worker-friendly regulations, which were widely discussed. But they uniquely included skill within their interpretative framework, placing employer support for skill formation on an equal footing with other cherished worker benefits and protections, including family-supporting wages, health insurance, paid leave, and job security; skill development was framed as part of the bundle of internal practices associated with well-paying jobs and career advancement opportunities. While these institutionalists were cautious not to overprivilege skill in the analysis, they did ensure it was recognized as a critical and valued component of decent work, and thus worth fighting for by labor advocates.

### Pushing Skill to the Side

There is little doubt the institutional structure of the US labor market continues to evolve in ways that further erode access to well-paying, high-quality jobs.[32] Still, while many US labor scholars agree on the extent of this institutional transformation and its role in intensifying employment and income instability, there is a visible splintering in how contemporary institutional analyses treat skill in relation to job quality gains or losses. And while the terms of this debate might at first seem overly technical and thus limited to academic interest, a closer reading is helpful for informing workforce practice as well, revealing prospects for action in support of institutional reconciliation and rebuilding.

Admittedly, for some institutionalists, skill remains critical to questions of institutional influence and thus recommendations for institutional rebuilding. And these scholars—many with faculty connections to MIT's Institute for Work and Employment Research—have inspired a network of researchers, myself included, to deepen our understanding of specific industry and sector trends in order to explore varying institutional arrangements that support (or, alternatively, undermine) skill development opportunities.

A recent illustration is a rich and detailed study of retail employment by Françoise Carré and Chris Tilly.[33] Using interviews with workers, employers, and retail experts in half a dozen nations, they captured important sources of variation in skill development strategies at both the national and corporate level. In particular, they found that retail firms and grocery chains throughout Germany benefit from a highly skilled workforce, with more than 80 percent of German retail workers completing a multiyear vocational education program, which can include retail-focused apprenticeships. By contrast, retail workers in the United States and United Kingdom experience little in the way of formal retail sector training, whether on-the-job or off-site. Carré and Tilly attribute some of this difference to national workforce policy, which helps explain why Germany has strong employer involvement in vocational training: it is actually required of them! Still, they draw attention to variation in employer-led training strategies, especially in liberal market economies, where state- or federal-level labor market policies have less impact. In the United States, for example, they feature several prominent American-based corporations—household names like Costco and Trader Joe's—that invest heavily in workforce training and related job quality commitments not because they are benevolent corporations but because they recognize there is productive value in doing so.[34]

But for many other contemporary institutionalists, skill has little place in America's evolving story of labor market transformation or the solutions necessary to improve job quality today. For these institutional scholars, the focus first and foremost is on federal and state regulatory structures, and not simply on factors that continue to threaten their existence but also on emergent legal and legislative openings for strengthening enforcement of antidiscrimination laws, higher minimum wage guarantees, required employment benefits (i.e., health insurance, family leave, and overtime pay), and related income-stabilizing legislation, such as the earned income tax credit.[35] These scholars not only stress the importance of targeting regulatory action for holding all firms accountable to high wage standards, they also emphasize its essential role in protecting workers against employer abuse and discrimination—protections that are especially needed by low-wage and immigrant workers at the bottom of the labor market.[36] Broadening their scope, some scholars have advocated for the creation of new federal institutional protections, drawing inspiration from European nations to propose a federally enacted social safety net that not only addresses worker needs but also aligns well with business desires for employment flexibility.[37]

While scholarship in this vein reinforces the call for high-level state and federal institutional action, it often does so by downplaying processes of institutional change *within* firms, especially those linked to the development of skill. Scholars hewing to this vein are less sanguine about skill development and make little attempt to link concerns over stagnating wages or declining job quality standards to the question of who does or does not have access to skill development opportunities. Some even take the argument a step further, claiming that policy or advocacy efforts that focus on workforce training and skill development are misguided and risk diverting attention from supra-organizational regulatory structures that mandate higher wage standards and codify stronger worker rights.[38]

The orientation away from the intrafirm practices of skill development is somewhat understandable, given the proclivity of American-based firms to take advantage of regulatory gaps to intensify worker vulnerability. We see strong evidence of this in the growing use of nontraditional work arrangements, including questionable forms of subcontracting, that reclassify workers as self-employed independent contractors despite restrictions on their actual independence (Uber drivers are an example).[39] Nontraditional arrangements also include the long-term use of temporary employment contracts and an "on-call" workforce that has no guaranteed schedule or claims to predictable earnings. And while "alternative work" arrangements still represent a small slice of all jobs in the United States (fewer than 20 percent of jobs, according to recent estimates), the numbers are on the rise.

According to a recent study by Harvard economists, 95 percent of net job growth in the United States between 2005 and 2015 involved some form of alternative employment arrangement, with prominent companies like Uber, TaskRabbit, and a host of temporary staffing agencies contributing to this upward trend.[40] In his 2014 book *The Fissured Workplace*, David Weil points especially to loopholes in federal employment law that encourage US firms to shift more workers from standard employment contracts to these alternative arrangements and, in the process, circumvent established employment-related benefits and wage guarantees.[41] By extension, the proposed solution to this emerging labor market problem is through regulatory channels.

A related trend with clear regulatory implications is the growing influence of financial investors, including private equity firms, that take control of company decision-making—a phenomenon commonly referred to as financialization. According to research by Eileen Appelbaum and Rosemary Batt, prominent investment firms often use their financial clout to reorient corporate strategy so that "activities designed to enrich shareholders" gain dominance over those that encourage innovation, productivity, and job quality, with a resultant scaling back of employer-sponsored training.[42] In keeping with studies that raise concerns about the proliferation of nonstandard work arrangements, scholarship on the labor side of financialization also encourages a decisive regulatory response—in this case, a series of ambitious national policy recommendations to "curb" the power of financial investors, including reclassifying private equity firms as employers so they can be held accountable for the damages they inflict on working America[43]— changes that were more within reach during the Obama administration but that could be advanced through progressive federal leadership.

But it is not simply the rise in nontraditional employment or financing arrangements that has led contemporary institutionalists to focus on regulatory reform and oversight. The presidency of Barack Obama helped catalyze this trend, opening channels for scholars and activists to inform federal action in support of worker protections and worker rights. During the Obama years, the White House frequently cited research by labor scholars and analysts in order to justify a series of worker-friendly actions around overtime pay, wage protections, and mandated worker benefits, including guaranteed health insurance. Labor and industry scholars were also appointed to influential federal agencies and advisory groups to shape and oversee policy implementation under the Obama administration; a notable example was the appointment of then-Boston University professor David Weil to the Department of Labor's Wage and Hour Division in 2014. And while attempts to boost the federal minimum wage ultimately failed to materialize under Obama's leadership, a series of academic studies did help support the steady adoption of higher minimum and living wage standards at the state and local level.[44]

Yet whether a response to intensified labor market restructuring or to a more hopeful, if short-lived, period when federal agencies were committed to pro-labor regulation during the Obama years, the outcome is the same—a widening chasm within institutional scholarship, with skill a defining edge. For some, this might seem a conceptual stretch: after all, early institutionalists, much like their counterparts today, strongly emphasized actions to strengthen supra-organizational institutions, including boosting labor union representation and advocating for pro-labor legislation and progressive taxation policy. But what is increasingly overlooked by today's institutionalists is the other side of the institutional coin: labor practices and processes within firms that reflect employer commitments to skill formation, with formal management strategies in place to closely link career mobility to wage increases, greater employment security, and improved job satisfaction.

For originating institutionalists, the regulatory structures outside the firm and the micro-institutional practices within them worked in unison to produce "mutual" benefits for industry, worker, and society alike.[45] Equally, early institutionalists helped demonstrate that external institutional protections both shaped and were shaped by sources of worker power often derived from the daily struggle over skill, including its development and resulting rewards.[46] In this respect, they were also cognizant of ongoing tensions between workers and employers, including less-than-ideal business practices that threatened this institutional harmony.

Given this earlier framing and its critical importance in reshaping the national debate over income inequality in the nineties, what should we then make of this current institutional divide over skill, and especially the turn outward, away from the internal workings of the firm? Should we assume that interdependencies that once were forged within and outside the firm are no longer attainable in our modern labor market environment, thus limiting options for institutional engagement to the formal, regulatory sphere? Or is there renewed opportunity for institutional integration that recognizes and draws out sources of labor power by engaging the microprocesses and micropolitics of skill—with added urgency to reclaim this institutional space in light of growing threats to worker-supporting regulation?

The case for reconnecting employer commitments to skill development with job quality standards has only gained in importance with the ascendency of President Donald Trump and his agenda to reverse Obama-era actions in support of worker rights and protections. Trump's selection of conservative US Supreme Court justices moves the antiworker dial further, with the potential for a more conservative court to stall progressive regulatory action for years if not decades to come. Furthermore, Trump's victory has emboldened conservative state leaders to roll back labor legislation and intensify efforts to derail labor union influence, especially undermining unions' ability to advocate for public sector employees and those trapped in precarious and nontraditional work arrangements.

Disheartening as they are, Trump's institutional attacks have also motivated labor leaders and worker-supporting organizations to search for novel and innovative strategies in support of job quality and worker rights. And it is here that skill development takes on a pivotal role, offering institutional inroads back into the firm, and with them, a means for labor advocates to push employers to embrace more encompassing job quality standards.

## The Soft Power in Skill Ambiguity

To illustrate this institutional potential, it is useful to first ask what is meant by skill, and, building from that, consider what is at stake for labor advocacy when concerns about skill are stripped from the job quality equation. As a starting place, it is important to recognize that skill is inherently ambiguous. That is to say, skill is fluid, hard to pin down, and subject to differences in interpretation.[47] This claim might strike some readers as problematic and out of step with contemporary employment dynamics, especially in light of recent efforts by labor scholars and related practitioners to motivate employer commitments to workforce development by seeking *more* precise measurements of skill.[48] But a closer look at studies of skill formation reveals not only considerable disagreement over how skill is defined but also starkly different perspectives on what constitutes a skilled worker—or, for that matter, a skilled job. These differences and related discrepancies create an opening for workplace mediators to engage employers around skill: there is power to this ambiguity that can be mobilized for increasing employer support for skill development and ultimately for tethering those commitments to other job quality gains.

To some extent, ambiguity around skill can be attributed to variation in research design, specifically differences in how analysts, including business consultants, operationalize skill.[49] Is it highest grade completed, number of years on the job, number of certification credits obtained, or something else entirely? As one example, surveys of employers—a common tool for assessing industry skill requirements—rarely generate consistent lists of which types of skill sets are most valued within an industry and which skills may be in short supply.[50] Some survey results emphasize the need for highly specialized technical skill, while others focus instead on general education requirements, especially basic math and reading comprehension. Still others feature a set of work habits and interpersonal and communication skills, or what are commonly referred to as "soft skills" or subsumed in the rubrics "career-readiness" or "employability." These differences are not just the result of occupational variation; they surface in studies of similar occupations and job types.

Not surprisingly, this inconsistency has led some labor scholars to call for improved survey design, with related recommendations for better data collection and coordination.[51] But there are limits to these data-focused solutions insofar as sources of skill ambiguity do not derive solely from data conflicts or misspecification. Rather, they stem from the *context-dependent* nature of skill, meaning it is very hard to separate skill from the social relations and work-based environments in which it is developed and deployed. In fact, this contextual element of skill makes it nearly impossible to generate a single, universally recognized metric other than a short list of rudimentary requirements.[52]

Theories of situated knowledge have long reinforced the grounded or context-dependent nature of skill.[53] As labor sociologist Paul Attewell points out, "Features of the context in which the work is done play a very important role in how the work is done, such a large role that it is meaningless to talk of a particular skill outside of the situations and practices in which it is used."[54] In other words, skill is not a set of fixed capabilities that workers carry with them to all work settings and environments, nor can it be reduced to a descriptive list of requirements for a given job.[55] Rather, skill is "situated" in the work environment itself and results from a dynamic and ongoing interplay between workers and their day-to-day work—that is, how they experience and come to understand that work.

This contextual side of skill underscores the need to recognize competencies that are produced through a variety of channels and experiences, only some of which depend on a traditional classroom format.[56] This line of reasoning is also useful for explaining why individuals often underperform in formal testing environments that differ significantly from the actual setting in which the skill sets being tested are initially developed or applied.[57] In an especially illustrative example, one study documented the use of sophisticated math and accounting techniques by children living in Brazil's high-poverty informal settlements or favelas. Their improvised techniques supported essential income-generating activities for their impoverished families, including begging or informal street vending, but also involved skills that were not easily transferred or reproduced in a traditional school or test-taking environment.

Similar differences have been observed among carpentry workers in South Africa, whose applied measurement systems depart from established industry standards but nonetheless generate high-performance buildings and structures.[58] And this variation is not limited to marginalized groups that lack access to basic educational supports. Harvard education scholar Houman Harouni provides compelling evidence of the coexistence of different forms of math that have evolved over the centuries to reflect their different applications, be they artisanal, philosophical, or, in the past few centuries, to support Western-based forms of business accounting and market transition.[59]

This constructivist framing of skill extends beyond individual mastery. It also helps bring to light sources of skill that are collectively rather than individually produced—skills that stem not from or through individual action but rather from the combined knowledge that is created and re-created in a group setting or team-based work environment.[60] Relatedly, context-dependent perspectives can uncover sources of "tacit" skills that remain hidden or obscure to the naked eye and whose broader relevance to those possessing the skill might be difficult to fully articulate to persons outside their core team.[61]

In his analysis, Jörgen Sandberg uses the term *interpretative* to capture contextual elements of skill and skill development.[62] As he emphasizes, workers gain skills and related competence through their ongoing *interpretation* of work. To use his own words, skill "is not primarily constituted by a specific set of attributes. Instead, it is based upon the workers' understanding of work." In contrast to rationalistic approaches, which define skill as a set of universally applicable attributes, Sandberg argues that skills "do not have fixed meanings, but rather, acquire meanings through the specific way that work is conceived."[63] As workers develop a deeper connection to and understanding of their work, they not only create new combinations of skill, they also devise new approaches in support of skill development.[64]

From Sandberg and others, we learn that workers reinterpret skill through their daily work activities and interactions. But there is another influential set of actors whose interpretive framing of work-based skill also matters: employers and supervisors who command authority over the work environment and have the power to officially support and sanction skill formation processes within it. From their position of authority, they can potentially interject a deeper understanding and appreciation for work processes and thus enhance the way that skills are developed and deployed by the workers they supervise. The opposite is equally true: they can introduce inconsistent understandings of skill from that of their workforce and ultimately add friction and uncertainty around skill.[65]

Why might this difference in skill interpretation matter? To start, it can generate deep-seated tensions around skill that can negatively affect the work environment, and with it undermine firm performance—a point I revisit in chapter 3. Furthermore, with conflicting perspectives in play, especially when one group has power over another but does not share perspectives, existing sources of workforce skill (including informal skill development processes that workers use) might not be adequately recognized or rewarded.[66]

With this tension, however, there also comes an opening for institutional engagement—and more specifically, for worker advocates to step in to resolve underlying differences in the interpretation of workforce skill. In the right institutional hands, skill-related ambiguity and conflict can drive job-improving negotiations and strengthen worker bargaining power by drawing out and better defending the skills workers deploy and develop at the worksite. To borrow a concept initially used in foreign policy analysis, there is "soft power" in skill ambiguity that can be useful for pushing employers to reinterpret their core assumptions not only about the value of skill but also about who possesses it and where it resides.[67] And equally, those negotiations around skill can be useful in convincing these same employers to share greater responsibility for skill development and helping them also recognize there is added value for their businesses when they nurture and sustain skills in the workplace.

But it is not just contemporary institutionalists that are focusing on the trade-offs and tensions that can inform how much employers are willing to commit to skill development. This issue is core to a branch of neoclassical economics created in the 1960s by the University of Chicago economist Gary Becker called human capital theory. And a brief review of that influential theory helps illustrate the limits to a fixed, rather than fluid, conception of skill. For Becker, the solution to getting more employers to upskill their workforce is quite simple and requires little in the way of (nonmarket) institutional intervention; it boils down to the type of skill that is in play. According to Becker's theory, if skills are "specific" to a firm—that is, if they are related to a particular set of tasks or systems that are unique to that one firm—then the employer in question would have a strong inclination to shoulder the burden for skill by investing in on-the-job training. It is when skills are "general" in form, having multipurpose applications and thus useful for multiple employers, that employers will take a step back. In line with Becker's human capital theory, employers in the latter situation would ultimately push the cost of and responsibility for general skill development onto the worker, either expecting workers to invest in their own formal education before they are hired or, alternatively, to accept a significantly lower wage to compensate for on-the-job training.

For Becker, this wage-training calculation is further cemented by the ability of firms in close proximity to one another to offer higher wages to lure skilled workers from neighboring businesses.[68] This possibility acts as a deterrent for firms to overcommit resources to general skill development, as other firms then have the option to poach that skilled workforce by using money saved from not training to increase their wage offer for employees already trained by their competitor. Short of contractually obligating workers with general skills to stay within the firm that trains them—a requirement that is difficult if not legally impossible to enforce—the threat of poaching means firms will attempt to pass along most of the cost and responsibility for general skill development to the workforce.

Assuming Becker is correct, could making skills more specific help shift greater responsibility for skill development to the firm? Is this where institutional action should focus? Not if we consider the analysis of other labor economists who have challenged the simplicity of Becker's specific versus general skill dichotomy in determining employer action. David Autor, for example, has sought to explain why temporary or third-party staffing agencies in the United States might offer general skills training.[69] According to his analysis, these agencies are not doing so just because they are positioned to pass along that cost in the form of lower wages for trainees. Rather, control over training functions as a powerful screening mechanism, giving employment agencies additional information about job seekers and their potential qualifications. This information in turn gives them an advantage in serving a local and regional labor market, insofar as they can guarantee their clients a skilled workforce and also charge them extra for pre-employment vetting. Economists Daron Acemoglu and Jörn-Steffen Pischke have extended the argument further in a paper aptly titled "Beyond Becker."[70] They add an important institutional twist, pointing to the influential role of national workforce systems in determining the extent to which employers take on responsibility for general skill development. They ground their analysis in a comparison of firms in Germany and the United States, with German employers agreeing to notably high rates of general-purpose training because there is greater industrial support and training system oversight from national government agencies.

More than just drawing attention to noncompetitive dynamics within a labor market, these critiques lend further support to the interpretative view of skill presented earlier in this chapter, illustrating that responsibility for skill development, including the basic question of who pays for it, is not set in stone—nor is it based on a predictable formula that can be applied to all organizational settings and employment relations. Rather, the decision by employers to accept greater responsibility for skill development is itself contextual and can be subject to institutional influence, not just through "hard" forms of regulatory action but also through "softer," microlevel institutional engagement that can alter how employers interpret skill and how they come to value its contribution to their own business success and the broader economy at large.

## Labor Market Institutions and the Defense of Skill

Worker advocates, most notably labor unions but also civil rights groups,[71] have long positioned themselves as defenders of work-based skill and have also engaged inconsistent interpretations around skill to deepen their labor market influence. But how they do so has differed considerably across industry lines and has also changed with time. A brief review of some of this history not only reveals what can be achieved when labor market institutions negotiate around skill, it also provides context for the remaining chapters of this book, which feature more contemporary negotiations by workforce institutions and intermediaries.

In the US construction industry—an industry I have studied in depth with my longtime collaborator, Natasha Iskander—building trades unions formalized employer commitments to skill development through industry-sanctioned apprenticeships, which the unions also tightly controlled.[72] While the bulk of new worker training received through construction apprenticeship programs occurred at the jobsite and often involved informal learning processes, there was considerable specificity with regard to required hours of training and how phases of training, once completed, would be compensated and rewarded. Union-friendly construction companies supported this formalized training structure by assigning skilled journeymen to support apprentice mentoring and by allowing a specified number of apprentices to work at each jobsite.

In contrast, the role of US labor unions in demonstrating and defending worker skill in manufacturing has been less direct. Outside the automotive sector, formal apprenticeship programs in US manufacturing have been quite rare, and those that existed—at least before President Obama launched his ambitious apprenticeship initiative in 2014—were limited to a handful of specialized occupations, such as tool and die maker or airplane mechanic. Reflecting this lacuna, union wages in manufacturing have been tied less to skill "mastery," such as we find in construction, and more to number of years worked in the industry.[73] While one could argue that seniority functions as a de facto signifier of skill, historical accounts of labor relations in manufacturing suggest a potentially different interpretation. Beyond a handful of specialized occupations formally recognized as "skilled crafts," most manufacturing jobs have been defined instead as "semiskilled," regardless of the seniority level of those filling these positions.[74] This perspective continues even today, most evidently in descriptions of manufacturing jobs as "middle-skilled."[75]

The view that manufacturing requires less skill relative to other manual trades appears to be unique to the United States. In western Europe, where labor unions have long represented manufacturing workers, there is considerably less differentiation. In Germany, for example, apprenticeships not only are commonplace in both manufacturing and construction but even today are structured and revised according to government-sanctioned educational and skill standards.[76] In Britain too, labor unions have long promoted manufacturing workers as highly skilled.

Why have manufacturing skill requirements been portrayed so differently in the United States? Are these jobs substantively different from their counterparts in Europe and therefore might require less worker intellect and skill? Some comparative accounts of manufacturing imply this might be the case.[77] Others suggest instead a more complicated institutional story that is not simply about identifiable differences in the organization of production or in how US workers relate to technology but rather reflects a long-standing struggle over the control of skill and its determinants.[78]

History is replete with examples of US employers and managers treating their manufacturing workforce as less skilled than it actually is.[79] Some accounts portray managers as woefully ignorant of the existing knowledge and skill that manufacturing workers bring to their jobs and further develop as they encounter complex problems at work.[80] Tom Juravich's rich ethnographic study of an electrical-wire-making plant in New England not only illustrates this point but also highlights the way that managerial ignorance can manifest in subsequent decisions that undermine channels through which workers share knowledge and collectively solve problems. Other accounts are less benign. Some labor scholars argue that US managers intentionally "deskilled" tasks by applying principles of scientific management, a.k.a. Taylorism, and by introducing a detailed division of labor that lowered skill requirements for most manufacturing jobs.[81] Doing so allowed managers to retain control over the labor process by creating an easily replenished manufacturing labor pool, and in this way made credible their threats to replace workers who resisted this structure or attempted to collectively organize against it.

Still, claims of purposeful deskilling by US managers are complicated by conflicting accounts that show managers' equally strong desire to engage worker intellect and ingenuity, including at the shop floor level.[82] Assumptions of widespread deskilling are further undermined by detailed studies of shop floor practices whereby manufacturing workers themselves created and willingly reproduced training systems, even after their employers officially withdrew support.

In the late 1960s, Peter B. Doeringer and Michael J. Piore, in their seminal book on internal labor markets, identified not only the informal processes through which manufacturing workers develop skills on the job but also workers' simultaneous efforts to conceal such practices from their supervisors. "In some cases they [workers] also have a strong incentive to hide what they do from management who might use this knowledge to extract greater output from them or to correct a loose incentive rate."[83] Building on this observation, Michael Burawoy's book *Manufacturing Consent* painted a rather troubling portrait of a complex power play between manufacturing workers and managers over skill and work responsibilities.[84] While Burawoy concluded that manufacturing workers were pawns in a rigged and unfairly structured game, he also observed that skill was a contested concept and open to interpretation.

Though such observations and analyses became widely known, at least through the late 1980s, US labor unions made few attempts to alter the perception that US manufacturing jobs were semiskilled, not highly skilled. Some of this reticence in requalifying jobs reflects unions' own legacy in specifying and reinforcing these differences in the early twentieth century, when union jobs were initially categorized as either "craft" or "industrial," with the former treated as highly skilled and the latter as semiskilled.[85] Labor unions fought among themselves over these classifications and what they implied for labor market jurisdictions and control. But long after this internal conflict had subsided and craft and industrial unions had united through the merger of the American Federation of Labor and the Congress of Industrial Organizations into the AFL-CIO, there still remained little need for "industrial" unions in the United States to explicitly challenge entrenched definitions of skill as long as manufacturing job growth remained robust and wage-setting processes remained in place to reward workers for years of industry service.

The picture changed in the late 1980s, when deindustrialization and intensifying threats from global competition ultimately pushed US labor unions to make a stronger case that worker skill was a central contributor to productivity gains in US manufacturing. At the forefront of this effort by industrial unions to wrest control over and better defend the skill of manufacturing workers was a novel American experiment (though admittedly one that drew heavy inspiration from Japan) called the high-performance work organization.

In its idealized form, the high-performance work organization that was popularized in the 1990s involved a range of company-supported human resource practices that were designed to increase the participation of rank-and-file workers in product and process innovation.[86] These practices included the use of more flexible work routines that allowed workers to move more freely across traditional job categories and, in the process, engage with, learn from, and combine multiple tasks. As this description implies, job rotation was a key element, as were open channels for communication and collective problem solving that crossed the traditional labor-management divide.

US manufacturing firms, especially those in automotive manufacturing, were early adopters of the high-performance model.[87] The United Auto Workers (UAW), the main labor union representing workers in the US automotive industry, was an especially eager participant, and as such, was prepared to relax traditional systems of seniority and rules of job allocation in order to support a more fluid work environment. The UAW worked closely with General Motors to introduce high-performance models at Saturn's production facilities in Tennessee and at the New United Motor Manufacturing, Inc. (NUMMI) plant, a joint venture with Toyota, in Fremont, California.[88] The UAW also worked with Japanese automotive manufacturers, especially Mazda, to incorporate high-performance elements at US-based assembly plants.[89]

In light of this commitment, labor scholars initially rejoiced in the high-performance experiment, viewing it as a new internal structure for engaging and valuing worker skill and ingenuity and linking those characteristics to improvements in job quality.[90] Further research, however, revealed potential limits to high-performance strategies, in particular the tendency toward only partial adoption within manufacturing and other sectors.[91] While a handful of US manufacturing facilities, namely GM's Saturn and NUMMI plants, adhered closely to the model's core principles and tenets, the vast majority of firms that classified themselves as high performance implemented only select elements of the model. And the procedures that did get implemented often had the perverse effect of increasing worker stress and turnover and foreclosing channels for skill development that high-performance work systems were meant to support. This situation led to claims by some labor market scholars that high-performance firms were also adopting "low-road" labor practices, which in turn undermined job quality and job security.

Interestingly, labor union involvement was often a determining factor in whether or not a firm adopted a more worker-friendly version of high performance.[92] Comparative studies in manufacturing noted that high-performance companies with strong union representation were also more likely than those without it to prioritize investments in worker training and to take steps to ensure shop floor workers were given sufficient time and resources to learn, master, and apply newly acquired skills and knowledge.[93] Without this institutional check, employers tended to underinvest in worker training and by extension to undermine the ability of their labor force to leverage skills for ongoing productivity gains and innovation. In this regard, unions formalized the links between worker skills, productivity, and job quality and ensured gains from high-performance strategies were shared among employers and employees alike. They also helped make visible the skills contribution of shop floor workers and defended formal structures and training investments that would ensure manufacturers continued to value and leverage this contribution.

In summary, US labor unions have constructively used skill ambiguity in past decades as a resource for pushing employers to commit to and sustain systems in support of work-based learning and career development. They continued this effort through experimentation with high-performance work systems and other novel labor-management agreements, tethering improvements in productivity to broad-reaching structures in support of skill development, including cross training and job rotation. With these arrangements, unions were not simply reinforcing industry skill demands; they actively contested employer attempts to appropriate, control, and underinvest in workforce skill, often establishing protective structures that would guarantee workers access to extensive on-the-job training and winning assurances that those skills would be rewarded through wage progression and industry-recognized portable credentials. With these structures in place, unions moved workforce skill from simply an employer resource to a well-defended worker right.

Have these gains been lost as union membership and influence have declined in the United States, including within manufacturing? Yes, to some extent. But widespread concern over skill shortages among US manufacturing firms, a concern shared by their institutional allies and influential policymakers, creates an opportunity to reclaim this institutional space. Employers' desire for a more skilled workforce opens up the possibility for new institutional actors to step in, using their engagement with employers to help workers get access to work-based learning opportunities while also introducing workplace changes that ensure workers share the benefits of their skills contribution to business performance and innovation. These matters are taken up in the following chapters.

# 3 Mediating Skill

## Let's Not Waste a Good Skills Crisis

Skill has weighed heavily on the minds of US business owners and policy-makers in the wake of the Great Recession of 2008–2009. Media reporting since the Great Recession has been textured with foreboding accounts of persistent skill shortages that not only limit industry expansion but are presumed to place heavy constraints on national productivity, innovation, and competitiveness.

For the manufacturing sector, the focus of this book, a highly cited prognostic guidepost is a 2011 report published by the Manufacturing Institute in partnership with Deloitte Consulting that estimated that close to 70 percent of US manufacturing firms faced a "moderate to severe shortage" of qualified labor.[1] And concerns about this shortage are not just confined to the years immediately following the Great Recession. The same study asked employer firms to forecast future needs, noting that over 50 percent of US-based manufacturing employers anticipated facing intensifying skill shortages in the coming decades, due especially to worker retirement. More recent statistics only reinforce that 2011 finding, indicating that US manufacturing has a much older and faster-aging workforce than the national workforce average.[2]

Widespread claims of industry skill shortages touch a raw nerve for many labor scholars, especially the institutionalists featured in the previous chapter that have long been critical of the purported link between technological change and skills mismatch.[3] Armed with new data sources and sharpened analytical insights, labor scholars in recent years have added a compelling new twist to their counterclaims: the idea that American firms create their own labor and skill shortages because they are unwilling to pay sufficiently high wages to draw out underutilized talent and skill.[4] In this context, low wages mean job seekers with highly desired skills have little to no incentive to apply for, remain in, or relocate in response to job openings. The problem then is not a lack of skill but anemic and stagnant wages.

The implications of this wage-skill disconnect feature prominently in a thought-provoking documentary titled *The Red Tail* that I often show to students in my labor seminars. The film follows the story of Ron Koch, a highly skilled aerospace mechanic who loses his unionized job at Northwest Airlines but turns down an offer from a competing passenger airline that sets his annual salary at roughly half his original rate. Rather than accept this insultingly low pay, Koch chooses instead to pursue a financially riskier, though more personally rewarding, dream of becoming a chef, toying with the idea of eventually starting his own restaurant instead of returning to his occupational roots. One labor market analyst reiterated what is clearly at stake here: "Trying to hire high-skilled workers at rock-bottom rates is *not* a skills gap."[5]

The recommendation that US employers increase wages to attract qualified candidates is compelling and worth further pursuit by labor advocates. And it adds strength to nationwide advocacy and organizing efforts in support of higher wages, including the "Fight for $15" movement.[6] Still, viewed through an older institutionalist tradition—one that also makes room for more nuanced work-based dynamics beyond wage-setting practices— it is potentially reductionist. Put simply, the pay-more-for-skills logic, in isolation, reduces skill to a ready-made, prepackaged commodity that will magically (re)appear, given the right price. It also assumes that skill is context-neutral and individually held, such that firms can easily pick it up through hiring and absorb it whenever it is needed—in other words, treating skill as plug-and-play.

In the previous chapter, I presented an alternative interpretation, treating skill as a dynamic and shared resource. This take on skill recognizes the need for it to be replenished and updated with time. It also factors in additional gains for economic opportunity and social mobility when skills are collectively developed and enhanced through ongoing active employer support and investment. By extension, this reframing means we do not need to cede the concept of skill to the market or narrowly ascribe it to any single individual. Rather, we can claim skill as a social good, opening up possibilities for targeted institutional action and advocacy in support of skill development, especially in the workplace.[7]

But what should that institutional response look like in relation to US employers? There are certainly limits to institutions simply calling on more employers to accept greater responsibility for skill development;[8] if firms haven't acted already, why should we expect them to readily do so now? And even if periods of labor market tightening might compel some form of skill-related action, it is not clear this mechanism alone would generate the desired results, either at the firm, industry, or individual level. (As an illustration, in May 2019, when I drafted this chapter, our national unemployment rate had dropped to a historic low of 3.6 percent. And while it is true that some American-based businesses were responding back then by showing greater interest in workplace learning initiatives, including warming to the concept of apprenticeship, many more were struggling to adapt to the changing employment environment, with some contemplating ways to circumvent the pressures of hiring or worker retention entirely, either by automating critical jobs or by shuttering operations permanently.)

In light of these varied yet highly consequential responses, labor scholars and advocates must be prepared to accept that there are real constraints that can limit firms' commitment of greater resources and attention to workforce development. There is also too much at stake to leave decisions about skill development entirely to firms. If we want the relationship between work and skill to change in ways that expand access to quality jobs, we must also be ready to act in support. A critical first step involves increasing awareness of intervening strategies that can enable more American employers to stick to skill development commitments over time and in ways that serve more vulnerable workers and populations.

## Who's Taking Action on Skill?

Concerns about skill and job access are central to a set of contemporary labor market institutions that are commonly referred to as *workforce intermediaries*—organizations, both public and not-for-profit, that mediate the relationship between employers and employees with the primary goal of improving earnings and career advancement opportunities for less educated and low-income workers and job seekers. Early leaders in workforce intermediation include Kentucky's Mountain Association for Community

Economic Development, Detroit's Focus: HOPE, San Antonio's Project Quest, New York City's Garment Industry Development Corporation, and Milwaukee's Wisconsin Regional Training Partnership, all of which have been well documented by labor analysts in a myriad of published articles and informative reports.[9] While a handful of influential intermediaries date back to the 1960s and have deep roots in the civil rights movement, hundreds more joined their ranks in the late 1980s and 1990s seeking to extend support to disadvantaged and vulnerable economic populations, including in response to changing federal welfare policy that pushed hundreds of thousands of welfare recipients into the labor market with little assurance of securing a quality job.[10] Early intermediary pioneers sought to fill a critical service gap in support of low-income job seekers while also experimenting with novel strategies to improve job quality standards by offering a range of support services and technical assistance to promising employers.

Today, workforce intermediaries are estimated to number around a thousand, with large concentrations active in the manufacturing and health care fields; the health care focus continues to grow in response to projected industry expansion, while intermediaries initially turned to the manufacturing sector in the early 1990s to try to stem industry job loss. And though a small group of intermediaries (fewer than 10 percent) are divisions of influential labor unions or joint labor-management partnerships, the majority have launched through other kinds of institutional affiliations, either classified as community-based not-for-profit organizations or managed through educational institutions, quasi-public workforce organizations, or, in a few cases, industry- or business-led associations.[11]

By design, workforce intermediaries seek to enhance the employment prospects of low-income or disadvantaged job seekers by connecting them to educational and training supports, including certificate or degree programs offered through vocational schools and community colleges. Establishing linkages to formal training programs is the hallmark of intermediation. But many notable workforce intermediaries also strive to intervene on the employer or "demand" side of the equation. They position themselves as "dual-customer," seeking to support both employer firms and job seekers.[12] To boost employment outcomes, these intermediaries take concerted and coordinated action to better align workforce training supports with the needs of local businesses. They often do so by establishing relationships with a diverse group of local employer firms, using those connections to draw out shared industry or regional training needs and then partnering with educational and training providers to translate those needs into improved classroom instruction and curriculum design.[13]

But some intermediaries take employer engagement to yet another level, developing concurrent strategies that push employers to share some of the burden for skill development with educational institutions.[14] They do this not simply by asking firms to pay for a greater share of that education but also by helping to formalize on-the-job training systems and skill-enhancing career pathways within the firm. It is these intermediaries—ones that successfully engage firms in a negotiated process around skill and get them to accept greater responsibility for its development—that are featured in this book.

## The Art of Employer Engagement

Admittedly, employer engagement around skill development is not an easy undertaking; to quote one intermediary, "It is more of an art than a science." While many workforce intermediaries acknowledge they are well positioned to use their local business connections to secure employment for vulnerable populations, they often struggle to gain traction beyond the point of getting someone hired. In some cases, intermediaries do not know how to effectively support a firm that lacks capacity or interest in changing internal training structures or routines to enhance the employment experience.[15] Furthermore, intermediaries often depend on the sustained goodwill of local employers to make inclusive hiring decisions. As a result, they may hesitate to push employers beyond established organizational practices, fearing such pressure could backfire and jeopardize their employer network, and with it their ability to place future job seekers.

One intermediary, when asked to explain the organization's reluctance to overstep, acknowledged that when the intermediary encounters firms that are unlikely to improve internal dynamics, it defaults to informing the job seeker and then coaching that person to adapt to a less-than-ideal work environment. If negative reports about the firm escalate, the intermediary might stop sending new candidates to the employer altogether. Reinforcing this view, another intermediary explained that it is much easier to phase out new employee recruitment services than to get a company to change its internal practices in support of job candidates already brought forward.

What options exist for improving strategies of employer engagement? How can workforce intermediaries increase their influence over employer decisions to strengthen internal workforce development structures and practices? And especially, how can they convince employer firms that there is long-term value in creating an inclusive learning environment and protecting that investment in skill through related improvements to job quality?

I have posed these and related questions to workforce experts and practitioners within a group of US-based workforce intermediaries that I have studied since 2010. The featured intermediaries are Lancaster County Workforce Investment Board in Pennsylvania, Chicago's ManufacturingWorks and Manufacturing Connect, Pittsburgh's New Century Careers, Cincinnati's Partners for a Competitive Workforce, WIRE-Net in Cleveland (now called Manufacturing Works, but with no affiliation to the Chicago-based program of the same name, which closed in 2017), and finally the Wisconsin Regional Training Partnership. While they differ in location, longevity, and governance structure, these intermediaries share a number of common features. All emphasize manufacturing jobs, which means they are categorized as *sectoral workforce intermediaries*, defined by the National Network for Sector Partners as "regional, industry-focused approaches that improve access to good jobs and/or increase job quality in ways that strengthen an industry's workforce." Most target their support to small and medium-sized manufacturing firms, recognizing these firms often struggle most with work-related issues.

The organizations I have studied were initially created in response to perceived skill shortages on the part of manufacturing employers in their respective regional economies. Each has used its labor market position to engage US manufacturers in a set of negotiations around skill, with the specific goal of removing barriers to rewarding job opportunities and career advancement for individuals who lack higher education credentials. To paraphrase a common refrain repeated by several of these intermediaries: they meet firms where they are, but they *do not* leave them there for long. While a comprehensive review of the specifics of each intermediary is beyond the scope of this chapter, the next sections provide a narrative composite of the innovative and adaptive strategies they use to push manufacturers to change how they think about, and act in support of, workforce skill. Chapters 4 and 5 go into more depth on programs in Chicago, Illinois, and the state of North Carolina.

## Getting a Foot in the Door

For workforce intermediaries, employer engagement often starts with a focus on hiring decisions, aimed especially at coaxing manufacturing firms to cast a wider net when recruiting new employees. Key here is the intermediary's ability to match job seekers with employers through pre-employment screening and assessment services. In that capacity, however, intermediaries do not simply act as agents of employers, as most for-profit staffing agencies would do.[16] Rather, they meditate the hiring process to support less educated job seekers who might otherwise be overlooked and thus excluded from quality employment opportunities.

An essential step involves encouraging employer firms to stop making hiring decisions on the basis of how an applicant looks "on paper." Why? Because standard application formats, and especially the ever-popular single-page résumé, not only reinforce an educational bias, they often obscure valuable sources of expertise that may be hard to articulate or defend in writing. As one intermediary leader put it, with just the résumé, "you don't have a true sense of that person." Even more troubling, an overreliance on résumés or simplified application materials has been linked to unconscious or implicit bias, which can further disadvantage women and people of color.[17]

With these risks in mind, the workforce intermediaries I have studied help firms initiate a more comprehensive approach to recruiting prospective applicants. In most cases, this involves gathering data from multiple sources to generate a more complete skills assessment. What matters especially is inclusion of diverse voices, particularly representatives from the incumbent workforce who have direct and intimate knowledge of established production practices and organizational routines. By treating the existing workforce as subject or domain experts—from the first-line supervisor down to experienced shop floor workers—these intermediaries help firms capture technical insights across a variety of tasks and occupational specializations. They also bring multiple parts of the firm into the conversation, compiling the information they gather to create a more encompassing skills profile.

Ultimately this approach shifts the focus away from generic educational credentials, which often stand as "a proxy for what they [firm owners] think is a qualified worker." One intermediary leader described this process an "evidence-based assessment." Another explained, "What we're trying to do is get really specific about what competencies and skills you [the firm] need and how you assess those skills." Pushing the approach further, he explicitly asks firms, "Does a credential or a degree really assess those skills? Or are there other ways to assess skill based on experience?"

This iterative and grounded approach to conceptualizing skill stands in stark contrast to current human resource (HR) management practice. Peter Cappelli, in his influential book *Why Good People Can't Get Jobs*, has documented the increasingly restrictive nature of contemporary management strategies, including a growing reliance on software applications and algorithm-driven hiring systems that create unnecessary hurdles for applicants and often exclude qualified candidates not just because they lack the preferred educational credential but also because they fail to insert more popular search terms. Cappelli also finds that "cutbacks in most HR departments now mean that there is rarely anyone left to push back on the hiring manager's job requisition and say, 'Are all these skills requirements a deal breaker?'"[18] This missed opportunity has only worsened in recent decades as firms outsource critical HR functions to private businesses or outside consultants.

By contrast, workforce intermediaries lean most heavily on workers who actually do the jobs in question and who, as a result, have intimate knowledge of the applied skills and learning opportunities most associated with them. Building on this base, some intermediaries take steps to insert worker insights into application materials and testing procedures. At least one intermediary designs and administers customized tests that correspond to the tasks each employer wants candidates to perform. As one director emphasized, the knowledge used in designing these tests comes from walking around the shop floor and having in-depth conversations with the front-line workforce, then using those exchanges to "pull out the specifics about what they [job applicants] need to know in terms of math, blueprints, precision measuring, machine operating, machine set up, safety and so on and so forth." He also shared an example to illustrate how this interactive approach helps his organization build a more trusting relationship with employer firms: "We created a 100 question test, the company narrowed it down to about 50 and now we are their sole point of contact when you [as job seeker] apply." He also stressed the added gains from this strategy for improved wage setting, noting that a customized test often helps to "close the wage gap" by giving employers greater confidence they are getting the skills they pay for in a new hire.

But could this kind of customized assistance inadvertently restrict job access by creating even more onerous hiring and skills requirements? After all, a more "precise" list of desired skills could mean additional grounds for candidate rejection: if firms develop more detailed skills profiles, the bar for securing work could be set impossibly high—where is the "soft power" in that? In actuality, the goal of this effort is not to create a fixed or rigid list of definitive hiring requirements for each and every applicant, nor is it simply to help the firm better advertise a job opening by including a bespoke and thorough description of the required work. Rather, the intermediary's primary objective is to create a tool for guiding employers' interpretation of skill: for drawing out less visible qualifications of a workforce that has already trained on-the-job and from there, for convincing employers there is deeper value to extending an employment offer to promising job candidates the employer might otherwise dismiss or overlook.

To reinforce this connection, the workforce intermediaries I have studied also spend considerable time with job candidates themselves, teasing out tacit skills and sharing insights to help candidates draw attention to transferable experiences during the job interview process. In some cases, this is done through one-on-one coaching, allowing the intermediary to share the specifics it has gleaned from individual employers to help an applicant interpret what might be most valuable to share from their career history and what skill sets to draw attention to and highlight. The goal here is to help brighten the portrait of the job applicant by having them reveal multiple strengths. Many of these intermediaries do this in the context of a formal career readiness class—not one narrowly focused on refreshing academic basics, such as high school math or reading comprehension, or on developing applied technical knowledge, though most offer this kind of support as well. Rather, in small group settings, they help job candidates develop and hone techniques to enhance the job search: they provide pointers on how to research a company and develop questions to ask during an interview, but also how to initiate and "close" negotiations if offered the job.

Reflective of this dual support for both employers and job seekers, one intermediary talked with us at length about the "360" analysis he shares with firms for a given job candidate. He stressed, "I *never* want to leave it just at their résumé, very cut and dried—do they have it, do they not. That is why we always do the 'pros and cons.' We point out and highlight the good aspects, saying to [the employer] for example, 'Yes I understand they don't have 15 years' experience, but this *is* a transferable skill.'" He likened the process to information gleaned from a Carfax report: a mix of "data, specs and opinions." And while he was quick to acknowledge that, "at the end of the day, [the company] makes the decision," he also made clear that his job is to broaden the parameters under which those decisions get made.

Still, in pushing a more granular appreciation of skill, there is increased potential for gaps in technical skills or experience to surface during the review of any single job applicant. These workforce intermediaries are fully prepared for this outcome and use their standing with firms to draw attention to a subset of qualities that still make a candidate a strong fit for a given company. Often this entails convincing employers to rank order attributes, thereby creating greater maneuvering room for applicants with some gaps on that weighted list. One intermediary described this approach as creating a skills bundle, "which is basically a set of attributes or credentials that *if* an individual was brought to them today, [that applicant] would be given consideration [and get an interview]. ... What's contained on that list are a set of minimum criteria." But this same intermediary unpacks things further, nudging firms to identify the next "set of preferred criteria that would get you [the applicant] that consideration. And then another set—so if you came in with this, [the company] would really love you." The key lesson here is they are not pushing the latter two criteria as requirements or universal asks but rather are using this layering to establish more realistic expectations on the part of the firm, getting it to treat this list as an à la carte skills menu of sorts, both reflecting and better supporting a diverse applicant pool. With such a complete and comprehensive list, it becomes *impossible* for any one candidate to fully fit the bill; accommodations must be made. Emphasizing this reality, one intermediary leader noted, "I do see lightbulbs turn on and I do see eyebrows being raised— where ... employers say, 'Hmm, okay, that [larger choice set] opens up some degrees of freedom for ... hiring processes.'" In an ironic twist, these intermediaries create detailed skills profiles not to undermine inclusion—as one might expect—but to facilitate it through stronger advocacy in support of job seekers who have *some* combination, though not all, of the preferred list of qualifications.

## Readying the Workplace for New Hires

Ultimately, negotiations around hiring are designed to reinforce ambiguity in skill, enabling intermediaries to also send the message that employers need to prepare for and work to resolve skill gaps identified through the hiring process. Once intermediaries have helped employers transform their hiring needs into successful job offers, they turn to the harder task of helping employers change their organizational routines and practices to ensure the firm can support and retain these newly hired workers. Although this work is more hands-on and intensive, it relies on many of the foundational elements cemented during the initial hiring phase. At this stage in the employment relationship, the goal often pivots from softening initially rigid skill requirements to identifying problematic management practices that can undermine career advancement or, worse, lead a newly hired worker to hastily resign. And here too, ongoing conversations with a wide range of incumbent front-line workers prove critical, providing intermediaries with a collection of narratives from which to identify signs of worker dissatisfaction or deep-rooted tensions that can be targeted through further action.

One intermediary described this particular aspect of his job as a form of "hybrid" consulting that straddles business management and workforce development, where he looks for "trouble spots" within a company that can undermine worker retention. Drawing this out for us through a hypothetical example, he might say to a firm's owners, "I know that you want twenty people right now, but before we do that for you, you really have to look at your (insert name of department or shift) because there's high turnover there." And to make the implications palpable, he might then say, "Until that's corrected, I don't want to get you twenty good people and they all quit, because there is a [supervisor] problem with your third shift."

These conversations between intermediaries and existing workers, including those the intermediary has previously placed in the firm, offer a form of informational triage. Through these exchanges, intermediaries can better pinpoint the root causes of a problem, often down to a specific department or supervisor—including identifying the "small things ... that even they [the firm owners] don't see." Ultimately, this allows intermediaries to avoid blanket characterizations of the firm: rather than marking it down as a universally bad employer or dysfunctional organization, they can instead locate the actual source of internal tension and more accurately convey details about it to the firm's owners when explaining why this dynamic is problematic and therefore needs to be addressed.

Then these intermediaries act on this insider knowledge in tangible ways that go beyond "putting a Band-Aid on a bad situation." Some take their message of concern to the next level, making actionable threats to stop serving a firm until the owners or key decision-makers commit to real change. One intermediary acknowledged that "yeah, we have pulled the plug" in cases where companies were not willing to address an underlying issue. But he also acknowledged that "nine out of ten times they come back—whether it's three months, six months or two years." And he said some firm owners they reengage later will even admit "we could have saved a lot of time [by working with you], as we're still at square one."

## From Problem Identification to Training Solution

Flagging problematic workplace dynamics is relatively easy, but solving them can be a years-long effort that requires time, dedication, and resources on the part of employers. The workforce intermediaries I have studied are committed to staying engaged, working with employers to develop effective solutions to ensure the employment opportunities they create are longlasting and beneficial for all involved. And it is here that intermediaries push firms to commit resources and time to work-based learning and on-the-job skill development. In cases in which a supervisor or manger is initially identified as the primary source of workplace conflict, training will often start there, with the intermediary saying to the owner, "Hey, we've got to educate this guy on how to be a trainer, or this person on how to be a supervisor." Improved communication with shop floor workers is often emphasized from the start. One intermediary shared a notable example to illustrate why this can be so critical. In that case, a plant manager at a midwestern manufacturing facility had created an elaborate literacy training program after receiving a hand-written note from a group of welders saying they "couldn't read." Only after he implemented the literacy program did he discover the welders in question actually meant they could not read the *specifications* he had written for that particular production order because the company had switched to a new style of pen that would smear by the third shift. Drawing out the training implications of this example, the intermediary noted, "We find these mistakes happen often when you don't involve the workers and where the communication isn't as accurate."

But it is not just higher-ranked employees and supervisors that benefit from the learning opportunities that workforce intermediaries help to create within firms. The intermediaries I have studied are most committed to focusing resources and attention on entry-level and front-line workers, helping to establish or extend supports that can advance these workers to a higher occupational rung and income bracket. One intermediary leader reinforced the importance of this commitment, stating point-blank that "half my day is spent not on recruitment or new candidate development, but it's also incumbent worker training, career pathway development, sometimes apprenticeship—how do you get someone from the assembly department into the CNC department, into the maintenance department, into the engineering department?" In other words, they take action to advance entry-level or front-line workers within a manufacturing organization.

A critical step involves getting firm owners to recognize there is a pressing need to support workforce development through formal on-the-job training. Admittedly, several intermediaries work with some firms that already appreciate the value of employer-led training. As one intermediary leader explained, "The best companies that we work with are always saying, 'We have to train people internally, we have to move them up. We can't have them stagnating here at the entry level position or at the operator position.'" But these cases are not the norm; most of the firms they engage with—particularly early in their relationship—need institutional assistance to move to this enlightened state.

Intermediaries often initiate this work by inserting the topic of front-line worker training early on in their employer discussions around worker recruitment and hiring. To this end, they may use grounded skill assessment processes to get employers to recognize the inherent difficulties in finding an exact skills match through the marketplace. These assessments also serve the purpose of warming the firm to the prospect of using new employee training to round out workforce skill. Reinforcing this point, one intermediary leader said she explains to firm owners that the goal of hiring is *not* finding the perfect technical skills match but rather "figuring out who is a good candidate *to invest in*—who will work for a long time." In other words, hiring a worker who will remain at the firm and thus be open to learning new skills and refining them over time is the goal.

From here, intermediaries take additional steps to design and implement new employee training supports, including an orientation phase commonly referred to in manufacturing as "onboarding." Often these intermediaries have some capacity to directly train newly hired workers. Depending on what is required, this can take the form of customized training developed in close consultation with the employer and administered at a specific worksite; in other cases, training is provided through a preexisting program or curriculum that the intermediary has already created but will modify or adapt to address the needs of different firms. While these more standardized training supports are not designed to eliminate the need for employers to formalize on-the-job training, they are helpful in easing firms into that commitment by establishing a consistent knowledge base on which employer-led training and mentoring can build. In most cases, this pre-employment training is time-restricted, lasting a few days to several weeks—again, with the goal of jump-starting, not substituting for, work-based learning. However, if intermediaries focus on a highly specialized occupational niche within manufacturing, such as biomanufacturing technician, discussed in chapter 5, those "base" programs can stretch out over several months.

### Navigating the Myths and Micropolitics of Skill

The workforce intermediaries whose experiences are core to this chapter do not stop at getting people hired and then trained for a new job; they push their relationship with employers further to help them recognize the value of deepening their commitment to skill development. Most intermediaries do this by helping firms extend skill- and career-enhancing opportunities to their incumbent manufacturing workforce, not only to promote the steady progress of more recently hired workers beyond the initial onboarding period but also to include in training opportunities those who have worked within a manufacturing facility for many years. Still, convincing employers to dedicate additional resources to incumbent worker training is not something that happens overnight. Stressing this, one intermediary leader noted, "You just have to keep planting seeds and be patient." But more than just playing a waiting game, these intermediaries take additional steps to assist firms in building out more encompassing, employer-led systems for continuous work-based learning.

In some cases, this can be achieved by resurrecting a training or mentoring system that was once in place within the firm but has long gone dormant as the existing workforce matured or mastered requisite skill sets. In these cases, firm owners and more senior workers not only have a distant memory of that training that intermediaries can draw on for motivation, they can also help firms access residual elements that might remain in place, even if informally practiced through coworker exchanges. Intermediaries are prepared to offer or help secure funding support to encourage firms to reinstate these older training systems, providing a "catalyst to move something from the back burner to the front burner." But they also recognize that an injection of funding may not be sufficient in all cases, especially if earlier training protocols were inconsistently applied to begin with or now prove out of step with modernized production practices or new applications in technology.

Beyond shoring up existing yet incomplete structures, intermediaries work to erect entirely new training solutions, building them from the ground up. In these situations, they may find they must first confront deeply held assumptions and myths about skill development, not just to get firm owners to think differently about an individual worker and that person's untapped potential but to reinterpret skill more generally in relation to other demands on the firm. One common assumption that undermines employer investment in skill is a nagging concern that incumbent worker training will come at the expense of production needs. As one intermediary leader explained, "The loss of productivity is what gets in the way of true education in the workplace. Everyone is afraid and can't afford to stop producing." Left unchecked, this assumption can spiral into paralyzing fear, especially for smaller-sized manufacturing firms. Often these smaller firms are buried deep within extended manufacturing supply chains and as such have limited power to renegotiate production schedules vis-à-vis larger, more prominent clients.[19] For the smaller manufacturing suppliers there is indeed some risk that training demands could disrupt short-term production scheduling by diverting precious resources from daily or weekly production tasks—this association often reinforces organizational complacency around training, with concern that time spent training incumbent workers could result in lost revenue or, worse, lead to the eventual loss of an important customer.

A related belief, and one that acts as an additional impediment to employer-supported training, is the notion that neighboring manufacturing firms will "poach" or hire away workers once they have been trained. When intermediaries query manufacturing employers about their lack of internal training supports, many respondents parrot some version of "Well, if we train them, they might leave." Labor economists have long associated managerial aversion to training with interfirm competition for skilled workers. As noted in chapter 2, early human capital theories anticipated this response, also predicting employers would naturally shy away from work-based learning unless the knowledge developed was so "specific" to the firm that it could not be appropriated by other organizations.

But when they encounter firms' fears that other firms will lure away their newly trained workforce, the intermediaries I have studied do not concede to this theoretical logic or support the existence of a dividing line between firm-specific and general-purpose skill. Nor do they let paralyzing tensions between production and training go unchallenged. Rather, they respond to these common concerns by presenting employers with an alternative vision, one that reframes inaction around work-based learning as self-sabotaging: a generator of long-term costs for the company, a hindrance to innovation, and ultimately a contributor to workplace tension and dysfunction.

One intermediary said that, on hearing some version of "If we train them, they might leave," he will quickly respond, "But if you don't train them, they [the workers] might actually stay"—in essence, flipping the standard logic in order to stress the problems that can arise when an existing production workforce remains inadequately trained, with skill potential underutilized or left to languish. Magnifying the generative force of this counternarrative, intermediaries also establish a stronger connection between worker knowledge and improved production practices and techniques. As one intermediary leader likes to emphasize in his ongoing conversations with firm owners, "The most valuable asset ... is the workers who are handling the product." And adding to that, the intermediary also stresses, "We start off with the premise that investing in worker training and involving workers in some of the decision-making process is the wisest thing to do ... to take value in what the workers can offer from a floor perspective." Another intermediary leader puts it in more explicit anatomical terms: "No [worker] likes to leave their brain at the door."

Intermediaries find they can also persuade firms to embrace incumbent worker training by drawing out potential conflicts that emerge at the worksite between newly hired and well-established workers. This helps firms reimagine skill as contested terrain, thus requiring thoughtful solutions that bring diverse groups of workers together rather than pushing them further apart. To some extent, intermediaries mitigate tensions by engaging incumbent workers in the design and implementation of pre-employment training. As these intermediaries can attest, the participation of the incumbent workforce means that existing workers have a stake in the career success of those the company has more recently hired. Still, for this mutual support to take root, the incumbent workforce must already have skills that new workers will gain during onboarding, or at least possess complementary expertise that is highly regarded and valued by the firm. If there is a real or even perceived cognitive gap, with newcomers gaining greater skills advantages and recognition, then the incumbent workforce will likely view the new coworkers as a potential threat.

Stressing this possibility, one intermediary noted, "New employees need to learn ten times more than they used to back in the day." And because this evolution in skills requirements is often gradual, firm owners may not fully appreciate the need to refresh the skills of the incumbent workforce—an oversight most likely to be found in firms that have not had to hire new workers in many years. Intermediaries not only help these firms prepare a strategy should tensions arise, they also buffer against it by making it clear to management that the incumbent workforce desires comparable training, including access to contemporary skill assessment options to ensure their previously mastered skills are formally recognized and respected by supervisors and newly hired coworkers alike.

Once firms realize the need to extend skill development across the entire workforce, the next critical step is introducing training systems that reflect and reinforce incumbent worker knowledge and expertise. As with new worker training, the intermediaries I have studied have a portfolio of options at the ready to strengthen incumbent worker training capacity within the firm. In some cases, an intermediary will adapt a program that it originally helped the firm create to support new worker onboarding, tailoring it into an effective skills equalizer for incumbent workers while also expediting the process to accommodate skills learned earlier in their manufacturing careers.

## Extending Intermediation through Apprenticeship

Many of the intermediaries featured in this book have recently added apprenticeship to their employer engagement toolkit—and in doing so, they are aware of growing bipartisan policy support for this form of work-based learning.

As they promote apprenticeship options in their exchanges with employers, intermediaries often advise firm owners to reserve initial apprenticeship slots for their incumbent workers, using that early participation to establish a solid mentoring team to support later cohorts. This is not just an effective strategy for reproducing the system by "training the trainer," it is another means for improving shop floor dynamics by giving incumbent workers a greater sense of responsibility and purpose.

But apprenticeship is not just a tool for bringing new and existing workers together. Its growing popularity among workforce and policy decisionmakers, nationally and regionally, also points to an opportunity for scaling up intermediation. One pioneering program developed by one of the intermediaries I have studied is exemplary in this respect, the Wisconsin Regional Training Partnership (WRTP). What makes WRTP's foray into apprenticeship notable is the development of a nontraditional manufacturing apprenticeship that extends work-based learning opportunities to traditionally marginalized segments of production workers, women and workers of color.[20]

Apprenticeship has long existed in American manufacturing, offering a structured form of on-the-job training that is combined with some kind of classroom education or "theory-based" learning. Historically, however, US manufacturing apprenticeships have served a very narrow segment of the workforce, mostly White male workers who were primed through apprenticeship for lucrative positions in machining, mechanical maintenance, or industrial electrics.[21] These manufacturing "trades" apprenticeships typically required a lengthy training commitment on the part of both workers and firms, extending over a five- to seven-year period and involving up to 10,000 hours of structured work-based learning and mentoring. The price tag for the company can quickly add up to hundreds of thousands of dollars, reflecting not only years of training wages and benefits but also the costs associated with the required classroom education. Access to these exclusive apprenticeships has historically been closely guarded by labor unions or influential patriarchs within a manufacturing family firm—which, in the latter case, means the invitation to participate is passed down from father to son or nephew.

Breaking with tradition, WRTP recognized the need for a shorter and more accessible apprenticeship option to better support skill development and certification of the broader production workforce. WRTP was seeking a stepwise solution—not an alternative to well-established trade apprenticeships but rather an incremental step to move more workers closer to that option. Additionally, they wanted to create an on-ramp into the "skilled" manufacturing trades for women and workers of color. Stressing this point, a WRTP leader acknowledged, IMT "is not as many years, not as many hours in the classroom and it's a lot cheaper." But more than that, "This mid-level apprenticeship highlights the people who can show up every day, who can learn, who can work together well. And then they get advanced standing in the more advanced apprenticeships."

After gauging employer interest, WRTP launched its Industrial Manufacturing Technicians (IMT) apprenticeship program in February 2013. Though significantly shorter than most traditional apprenticeships in manufacturing, IMT is a federally registered program, meaning all sponsoring employers must adhere to a fixed ratio of on-the-job training and classroom education, and implement a wage progression schedule that is tied to specified learning objectives. Reporting on the underlying process of employer engagement that went into program design—which included a year of consultation with manufacturing firms—WRTP's Rhandi Berth and her co-authors from the Center on Wisconsin Strategy noted that "this process helped industry leaders realize that, despite greater specialization inside firms, the skills in short supply were similar across firms."[22] WRTP thus chose to create a blended model that transcends the boundaries of general versus specific skills, pushing multiple firms to agree to support industry-wide skills profiles while at the same time building in flexible training time for firms to support the development of "unique," firm-specific occupational categories.

The IMT program has proven extremely popular among American-based manufacturers, allowing WRTP to replicate it in four other states and enroll more than one thousand manufacturing workers as of December 2018. Here too the initial push came in support of incumbent manufacturing workers, with WRTP and its partners using the IMT program to first codify existing skills and elevate incumbent worker standing. But there are as well observable benefits for job seekers, including dislocated manufacturing workers, who are entering the program in increasing numbers to regain manufacturing employment. IMT apprentices earn four transferable credentials set by a national industry association, the Manufacturing Skill Standards Council, which also designs testing materials. By undergoing testing for certification, former manufacturing workers reduce the chance that entering a new manufacturing establishment will mean they are "treated like high school students … or like they don't know anything," as one interviewee put it.

With the IMT apprenticeship program—and most other work-based training solutions supported by these intermediaries—there is certainly a role to be played by external educational institutions, including community colleges and well-established vocational education centers. The various intermediaries I have studied explore options for bringing educational providers into the mix to support incumbent worker upskilling and administer industry-recognized certification. This institutional partnering helps employers gain greater appreciation for formal educational programs and works to establish a channel for "industry-recognized credentials" through employer involvement in curriculum design and program evaluation. Still, the goal for the intermediary in brokering the employer–educational provider relationship is not to blindly push the incumbent workforce into a stressful, expensive, or time-consuming college or university degree program or to tip the balance away from employer-led work-based learning. Rather, intermediaries use their institutional clout to provide firms and workers with a more complete roster of training and credentialing resources with a primary objective of making the hidden talents of the incumbent workforce more visible and valued.

### Advancing Job Quality

Up to this point, I have emphasized the role that workforce intermediaries play in improving workforce training within the firms they engage. But for intermediaries to make a real difference in economic mobility, they need to translate those learning opportunities into other types of income and job quality gains. Here too intermediaries are well positioned to leverage the soft power of skill to push those employer commitments even further.

Higher wages are an obvious target for intermediaries, reflecting their dual mission to strengthen firms while also enhancing the take-home pay of low-income workers or job seekers. Most of these intermediaries broach the issue of wage increases during their initial interactions with the firm. For at least two of the intermediaries I have followed, wages are also a key criterion used to determine whether and in what capacity the intermediary will agree to support the skill needs of prospective client firms.[23] If the intermediary finds wages are set well below its criteria for an acceptable starting wage, it will greatly curtail its menu of support services. If such a firm nonetheless demonstrates a genuine willingness to improve, the intermediary may leave open the option to steadily expand its support in order to ensure those wage requirements are met.

To reinforce the value of paying higher wages, these intermediaries often share aggregate information they have gleaned from other firms or industry-wide sources, using it to show more definitively that the firm in question is underpaying relative to its manufacturing peers. They use this same information to stress that paying a lower-than-average wage could result in ongoing worker retention problems, playing on fears that employers have around training but linking worker loss to factors within the firm's control. Emphasizing this wage–worker retention connection, one intermediary noted it shares industry data to make sure "companies are calibrating their compensation packages based on … reality." By serving multiple employers in the same industry and region, intermediaries are able not only to track incremental changes in average wages but also to establish a reference point for the value of extending other income-supporting employer benefits, including paid sick leave, child care, transportation assistance, and quality health insurance. In this respect, they are not just mediating the employment relationship at the workplace level; they are also using their position to "raise the bar" regionally by helping firms rethink their practices in comparison to other regional employers and sharing information on industry practices and up-to-date labor market data.[24]

But intermediaries are not focused solely on securing higher wage standards or more generous worker benefits. Their support for inclusive career structures, as well as better management and supervision, reflects a more holistic view of what constitutes a quality job: one with better pay and benefits, certainly, but also with job security, predictable scheduling, safety procedures, worker representation, and worker participation, among other criteria. They often raise these multiple factors during early conversations with firms, especially when firm owners resist investing in worker training out of concern that other firms might poach the newly trained worker. To help firms break through the inaction that results from such circular thinking, intermediaries return again to the internal dynamics that can result in a newly hired worker leaving for another job. In other words, they do not limit the discussion to the potential pull of a better wage elsewhere but broaden the conversation to take in additional stresses that might force a worker out, even if that worker's pay rate gets a big bump. Reinforcing this point, one intermediary stated that "if the firm really believes that working at their company is so terrible that a younger person who's starting their career is going to jump ship … that's something that needs to be tackled." Another intermediary, when encountering a firm that raises concerns that better trained workers will simply leave, is quick to respond, "Well, are the working conditions bad?"—a question asked with the dual intention of leading the firm to think critically about its overall working environment and getting it to see investments in its workforce, including training, as part of a larger job quality commitment.

The ultimate goal for the intermediary is to get the firm to recognize the deeper value in having a well-trained, happy, and financially secure workforce. With this in mind, these intermediaries push firms to continuously improve the work environment, drawing on insights about wider industry practices to suggest improved channels for worker input and decision-making, including opportunities for front-line workers to participate in process and product innovation. By offering ongoing recommendations, intermediaries also help firms send a more powerful message to current and prospective workers, namely, "We are going to invest in you, as we want you to remain here and be a valued partner with us [the firm]."

Importantly, these intermediaries recognize the need to include other influential voices in the mix to help reinforce for firms the benefits of a sustained commitment to work-based learning, improved pay, and good working conditions. They often solicit help from industry "champions," including committed manufacturers they have worked with and supported in the past. In small group meetings or through informal business mentoring channels, industry champions "talk to their peers about why [these workplace improvements are] a good strategy. How they helped them [the employer]. … How they improve productivity and job retention." Equally, these discussions are designed to stress gains for their "people—the employees; improved earning power and … stability in the labor market." In brokering these peer-to-peer conversations, intermediaries reinforce the mutual gains for firm and worker alike, with "both voices being amplified in the workforce development conversation—the job holders as well as the employer."

## Skill Reinterpretation

In summary, the intermediaries I have studied all engage in some form of skill reinterpretation; figure 3.1 captures the strategies and techniques that constitute this work. Intermediaries initiate the reinterpretation process by helping employers *reimagine* skill, starting with a qualitative examination of skill in the workplace. Drawing heavily on conversations with incumbent workers, intermediaries move employers and top-level supervisors through a cognitive shift, broadening their understanding of who may be able to fill vacant positions and who can bring value to the workplace. Then, as intermediaries help employers gain greater appreciation for less visible skills and transferable experience, they push them to realize where they need to *restructure* existing workplace practices to support ongoing skill development opportunities. This commonly includes instituting formal training programs and better supervision to foster new capabilities and nurture the nascent employment relationship.

The intermediaries whose views were presented in this chapter are acutely aware of the need to implement these two strategies in tandem, treating them as two sides of the same coin, equally vital to the ultimate

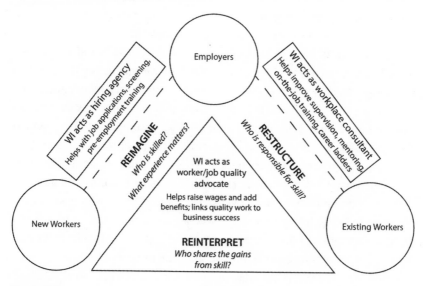

**Figure 3.1**
Skill reinterpretation strategies used by workplace intermediaries (WI).

goal of strengthening employment opportunities. Without shifts in perception, there is a high risk that firms will pass over job seekers and workers with lower levels of education. Certainly employers can formalize internal training structures without making much of a cognitive leap, but the structures they create are unlikely to reach far enough into the workforce to have an impact on income inequality. It is more likely these employers will continue to favor highly educated or more senior workers at the expense of others, reinforcing a polarized work environment that intensifies economic insecurity for workers at the bottom of the labor market. In this respect, the joint focus by intermediaries on reimagining skill *and* restructuring firms for skill development is critical for spurring economic mobility.

But intermediaries also use an important third strategy to iterate the connection between changing perception and changing practice: they engage employers in deep moral reflection over responsibility for skill development, in both immediate and long-term thinking. We see this play out in their ongoing challenge to standard representations of skill, making it less of an individual prerequisite to *secure* work and more of a shared common good that is produced and reproduced through collective and social processes *at* work. With this aspect of *reinterpretation*, skill and work become inseparable, and in further strengthening that connection, intermediaries set the stage for advocating greater improvements to work itself, even as they continue to push stronger skill development opportunities within it.

The ambiguity around skill is key to understanding—and enacting— these varying strategies of reinterpretation. As we saw in the descriptions of intermediaries' work in this chapter, intermediaries regularly harness the soft power devolving from skill uncertainty to push employers to critically examine, and ultimately revise, their starting assumptions about which skills are really required and at what point in time, a revaluation that in turn enables employers to become more open to a diverse set of job applicants and relatable work experiences. Intermediaries point to skill ambiguity in their ongoing discussions over skill responsibility, pushing employers to simultaneously interpret training as *both* a worker benefit and a workplace investment, ultimately making it less likely that employers will step back or renege on an earlier training commitment or its associated reward. But these intermediaries also play up uncertainty to push against standard categories of skill—including overly stylized concepts of specific versus general skills—which can mask superficial yet resolvable fears or constraints that can stop employers, especially smaller manufacturers, from making long-term investments in the workforce.

This is not to say these intermediaries artificially keep skill in a constant state of ambiguity: there are clearly moments when they work to reduce confusion around skill, as when they draw on the tacit knowledge of incumbent workers to articulate skill needs and workplace practices that may be poorly understood even by the employers. Nonetheless, these intermediaries recognize the motivational power of uncertainty to move employers beyond stasis and ultimately to inspire them to commit to skill development in meaningful and lasting ways.

## Ecosystems and Exoskeletons

Can more be done to expand skill-focused intermediation beyond the inspiring work described in this chapter? Steven Dawson, an influential thought leader in the world of workforce development and founding president of a highly regarded health care intermediary in the South Bronx, published a job quality briefing in late 2017 calling on American-based workforce practitioners and activists to take action in response to employers' "desperation for labor."[25] As he notes, the pressing need for skilled workers creates an even greater opening for workforce organizations, including more traditional educational institutions, to better "serve the mutual self-interests of both workers and employers"[26] and with it, to enhance access to quality jobs. The various intermediaries outlined in this chapter have long heeded this advice, taking advantage of periods of labor market tightening in the 1990s and 2000s to engage firm owners around skill and devise innovative solutions that also offer a portal for instituting job-improving transformational change within employer organizations.

But periods of low unemployment are often temporary. So does this mean the window for workforce intermediaries to negotiate with employers around skill will close in times of economic recession—a question made more relevant by the "pandemic" recession that started in spring 2020, when this book was complete and in production? Are there other institutional channels for shoring up workforce intermediation during weak labor market conditions?

The Workforce Innovation and Opportunity Act of 2014 added a forward-looking provision requiring states to allocate federal dollars to sector strategies, meaning that workforce funding needs to have a specified industry target and include structures to make public investments more industry- and employer-responsive. Workforce policy and technical assistance organizations, including the National Skills Coalition, have provided leading analysis in support of this federal policy change, and they continue to work closely with state officials to help diffuse sector-focused strategies. While this does not guarantee that all employers deriving benefit from this legislation will take action to improve job quality or agree to extend economic opportunity to low-wage job seekers, it does create a sanctioned opening for sector-based workforce intermediaries to work more closely with state and regional agencies to help implement and further innovate around this policy mandate.

Additionally, growing support for apprenticeship among elected officials of both major political parties—including at the federal level under both Obama and Trump—creates another channel for targeted intervention by new and established intermediaries. Apprenticeship is a natural platform for scaling up workforce intermediation because of the requirement that employers provide the bulk of apprentice training and structured supervision at the jobsite, effectively enabling more intermediaries to step in to aid employers in the design of those and related workforce supports. The workplace intermediaries that appeared in this chapter have acted in response to widening national interest in apprenticeship, with at least one applying to be the official apprenticeship sponsor on record. With this novel arrangement, they not only closely control the placement of apprentices across a network of local manufacturing businesses but also are well positioned to shape what on-the-job learning looks like within those work environments, and who benefits from it. Business interest in apprenticeship—along with continued federal and state funding for apprenticeship development—means that even with our national economy in recession, workforce intermediaries can augment their institutional visibility and offer to help firms adjust to more challenging economic circumstances in ways that also allow them to exert greater influence over employment-related decisions and actions.

Recognizing this, other labor analysts writing in this policy space have called on public workforce development agencies to better coordinate their activities at the state and regional levels in order to reach a larger segment of the working population, with the intention of creating a stronger institutional safety net.[27] Relevant activities include embedding intermediary-like structures within publicly funded community colleges, knowing these educational institutions can adopt many of the work-enhancing practices that are outlined in this chapter, and supporting organizational improvements through their small business assistance programs. For manufacturing in particular, there is growing recognition that workforce solutions can be grafted onto the federally funded Manufacturing Extension Partnership (MEP). Launched in the early 1990s, the MEP is a vast network of industrial extension centers that provides business and technical assistance to small and medium-sized manufacturing firms.[28] Every state has at least one MEP center that is funded through state and federal sources and charged with helping smaller manufacturers integrate modern technology or introduce organizational changes that enhance overall business performance.

The MEP's highly regarded business consulting and technical services, in combination with intermediary-like workforce development functions, have the potential to reach hundreds of thousands of manufacturing workers. While some MEP centers have already accepted this challenge and adapted their services to better support front-line production workers,[29] even greater growth potential could be realized from existing workforce organizations partnering with their respective MEP centers—in other words, partnering so as not to overwhelm the MEP with additional workforce requirements, but also using this cross-cutting alliance to bring manufacturing extension and workforce service providers into closer alignment. Insofar as each state hosts one or more manufacturing extension centers, this national MEP network offers a robust institutional platform for existing workforce advocacy organizations to reach thousands of small and medium-sized manufacturers annually served by MEP extension specialists. And the power of workforce providers partnering with the MEP is not simply a means to reach more employers. To borrow Steven Dawson's inspiring language, this connection creates the option to fundamentally "change the public narrative about employer 'success.'"[30] With the MEP providing a solid platform, workforce intermediaries could advance Dawson's proposed "paradigm shift," making the business case for extending economic opportunity to front-line workers and moving the conceptual goal post from narrow profit-making motives to a stronger business commitment to shared prosperity and mutually beneficial economic gains.

The term "ecosystem" is reflective of this larger push for workforce development to become boundary spanning; it has been used by a number of labor scholars of late to encourage workforce practitioners to forge closer connections to organizations across the traditional economic and workforce development divide.[31] An integrated institutional approach has the potential to knit together resources and technical expertise that might otherwise be applied in isolation or, worse, competition. The idea instead is to create an institutional force multiplier, not only to serve a larger number of employers and workers but to create a stronger coalition for building political support and guiding policy action—an approach that mirrors the reconceptualization of economic development as an adaptive and coordinated process for responding to emergent challenges and opportunities.[32]

But as we look to these wider institutional networks in hopes of enhancing the impact of workforce intermediation, it is important to focus not only on how these entities relate to one another or draw in other service providers, be they educational, community-based, or technical in nature. A well-mapped institutional ecosystem alone will not cut it, especially if that means only looking outside the firm to consider who locates and interacts within that externally networked institutional space. Rather, it is also important to carefully document the kinds of strategies that workforce intermediaries and their institutional partners develop to become more effective at employer engagement and ultimately to exert greater influence over business thinking and action within private sector firms and work-supporting organizations.

Workforce intermediaries are powerful not just because they forge partnerships with other external institutions. Their influence comes from building a workforce structure or exoskeleton around the firms they engage. With that effort, they certainly create an opening for bringing additional institutional support and advocacy to workers within those firms—though ultimately, they put in place adaptive and enduring workplace structures that reflect and reinforce employer commitments to support a better and more rewarding employment experience.

But just as ecosystems need to adapt in response to changing environmental conditions, so too must the exoskeletons that intermediaries build around the firms they engage adapt to changes. The intermediaries featured in this chapter have erected these structures initially to support adult workers and job seekers who all have prior employment experience and some kind of work-based learning on which to draw. But what happens when the workers in question are entirely new to the labor market, energetic yet inexperienced, eager yet less qualified? Here too, we find intermediaries taking the lead to lend young job seekers a supportive hand. Youth-supporting intermediaries are also focusing on skill as part of a broader job-centered strategy, and here again they stress that employers cannot afford to be passive consumers of externally provided training and education, even at the high school level. To strengthen the future of American manufacturing, employers need to step up and become co-creators of next-generation skills—and intermediaries are ready to coach them through that transition as well.

# 4 Skilling the Next Generation

A young employee pulls a smart phone out of his back pocket, checking for a new email or text message every hour or so during his eight-hour shift at a small manufacturing firm. This is not only a violation of official company policy but, by creating a shop floor distraction, it also poses a safety risk. At a nearby manufacturing facility, a young woman grows increasingly agitated, even angling "to [verbally] fight back" when her supervisor calls her out for failing to accurately log the number of parts she generated at her assigned machine, a step used to track the pace of production and recalibrate the company's lead time for future orders. At yet another manufacturing firm, a newly hired eighteen-year-old attempts to overhaul a well-established protocol with the assumption it will improve the production process, yet fails to solicit advice from his supervisor before implementing this critical change.

At first glance, these scenarios, drawn from conversations with young manufacturing workers in the Austin neighborhood on the West Side of Chicago, could be chalked up to youthful ignorance or immaturity: naïve acts, perhaps, or simply the result of overexuberance that will eventually resolve as younger employees grow in experience, time on the job, and age. But a closer look reveals that the fault is not theirs alone. In each case their employers and supervisors have made common missteps. In the first instance, the employer fails to explain or enforce company rules for personal cell phone or email use. In the second scenario there is a related failure to fully articulate why a particular task must be performed and reinforcing its importance by clearly explaining how it contributes to a larger production or delivery supply system. In the third scenario, there is a missed opportunity to capture and focus the creative imagination of a young employee, inspiring him not only to innovate and problem solve in real time but to do so in close consultation with more experienced and more senior coworkers.

Skipping these steps is not inconsequential. Unaddressed, each of these scenarios can lead to workplace conflict, igniting friction between incumbent and newly hired workers or between an older and a younger manufacturing generation. Worse still, they risk perpetuating racial inequality, as all three of these young workers are African American, and the older, highly experienced workforce they are joining is mostly White. Simmering tensions like these, if left unresolved, can be costly for manufacturing firms as well. They can undermine workplace morale and dampen the creative spirit of a youthful workforce, driving young workers to cognitively disengage or walk away entirely from potentially rewarding jobs.

How employers engage younger workers has long-term implications for a firm—but more than that, the failure to create supportive work environments for first-time workers threatens the US manufacturing industry as a whole, further undermining national and regional economic health. As concerns over staffing shortages intensify with the looming retirement of the boomer-age manufacturing workforce, the challenge of recruiting and retaining a younger, more diverse workforce to US manufacturing grows even stronger. According to a recent survey of 1,200 young workers in hourly positions, including in manufacturing, more than a quarter expressed deep dissatisfaction with their current employment situation and more than half indicated that they planned to quit their job within the year.[1] A recent meta-analysis conducted by the Center for American Progress estimates that the cost of worker turnover for entry-level positions is between 16 and 19 percent of the employee's annual salary.[2] Given that most entry-level manufacturing jobs pay between $30,000 and $60,000 a year, the center estimates the cost to replace an individual worker, which includes time spent on new employee screening and training, can be upward of $8,000.

During the Great Recession, some manufacturers found temporary relief by absorbing laid-off workers from other firms that had thinned their production ranks or permanently closed their factory doors.[3] This gave the hiring manufacturer access to a highly experienced and deeply knowledgeable production crew—a "plug-and-play" workforce requiring less on-the-job training. But with this source of pre-trained workers drying up and especially with a wave of retirements on the horizon, US manufacturers are under increasing pressure to develop alternative workforce solutions.

Hiring young job seekers is the obvious choice, and for some firms it is the only lifeline for filling long-term vacancies. If done well, the incorporation of younger workers, including workers of color, into manufacturing can also serve an important societal role, helping to lower youth unemployment and opening a pathway into the middle class that does not require immediate completion of higher education or the accompanying assumption of massive amounts of college debt.

But for this to happen, American manufacturers must take proactive steps to attract and support a younger generation of workers. This means signaling opportunities for career mobility and creating a robust learning environment in which young workers can develop and apply new skills. It entails modifying organizational structures to better augment and reward skill development, establishing well-illuminated career pathways with clear wage progressions. It might also require company support for higher education, including tuition reimbursement programs to encourage workers to pursue a college degree.

Despite the compelling case in favor of adapting to a younger, more diverse workforce, it is often difficult if not impossible for many US-based manufacturers to commit to these kinds of organizational changes without some form of institutional assistance. Small and medium-sized facilities in particular often struggle to introduce job-enhancing improvements, especially when they have dismantled internal training systems or outsourced key human resource (HR) functions. Smaller, less prominent firms must also contend with the legitimate concern that, from a job seeker's perspective, manufacturing is a dying sector offering limited career prospects for younger labor market entrants. The recent media frenzy over automation and related threats to manufacturing jobs have only magnified this fear, especially for anxious parents eager to see their children enjoy a prosperous and rewarding career.

How can US manufacturers attract a younger, energized workforce? What steps must they take to signal strong support for youth employment and career mobility? What skill-enhancing assistance can workforce intermediaries offer these firms, and how might they structure that support to benefit youth from low-income communities of color that have seen their own family members suffer from the ebb and flow of manufacturing employment?

### The Case of Manufacturing Connect

Manufacturing Connect (MC) in Chicago offers a promising model for helping employers nurture next-generation talent by extending career-enhancing opportunities in manufacturing to young job seekers.[4] The program was launched in 2007 as a high school elective and until September 2019 was physically embedded in two public high schools and worked with a third, becoming actively involved in day-to-day student advising and curriculum development and so providing a model for how a public school system can prepare and connect in-school youth to meaningful jobs in manufacturing. MC now works in a reorganized format outside the school system and is exploring the option of building a stand-alone training center through which to reach students and teachers across the public school system, expanding far beyond the three original pilot schools.

Even with this significant restructuring still in progress, the continuing goal of MC is to encourage youth in high-poverty, historically Black urban neighborhoods to consider careers in applied engineering and manufacturing. This is no ordinary vocational training program designed to simply track youth into manufacturing jobs. MC seeks to open up a full range of options for economically disadvantaged high school students and their families by providing a nested set of supports, including career and college counseling.

The program has helped lead high school students to rewarding manufacturing jobs, a focus that is discussed in greater detail later in this chapter. But it also ensures other options remain in play, including by planting the seed for eventual business ownership among the student participants. In this respect, the creators of MC recognize that economic opportunity is about expanding rather than constricting career choices. For MC, this also means ensuring participants have the option to pursue a two- or four-year college degree or to combine higher education with paid manufacturing work so that college enrollment remains affordable *and* career enhancing. More than half of MC's participating students enroll in college, which program leaders celebrate as a significant success.

In this respect, MC is not about etching a dividing line between higher education and employment, nor is it structured to force students to make stark choices now that cannot be reevaluated and shifted as they learn and grow. Rather, the program seeks to develop flexible, iterative, low-risk solutions that enhance income security and career advancement for economically vulnerable youth.

This chapter is not intended as a program evaluation or an assessment of MC's long-term sustainability.[5] Rather, it offers an illustrative case that shows how an intermediary that is designed to extend educational and economic opportunity to low-income youth can also bring about changes within firms in support of job access and career mobility. We observe in this case an early intermediary pioneer combining high-touch employer engagement with wraparound support services to help disadvantaged youth of color overcome significant barriers to accessing quality employment. It is the only program featured in this book that has an explicit and dedicated youth focus—yet the beneficiaries are not limited to youth participants and other young job seekers like them. The changes that MC staff have helped employers introduce and formalize are benefiting other workers, including incumbents with substantial work experience in manufacturing.

This chapter therefore offers reinforcing evidence that employer engagement around skill development is critical to ensuring all workers have access to a more supportive and inclusive work environment, including upcoming generations. But equally, there are lessons about institutional vulnerability that can be gleaned from this in-depth case study. As a nonprofit intermediary, MC is at the mercy of a large educational bureaucracy, the Chicago Public School system. MC's recent restructuring—one born out of necessity, not desire—reflects its precarious position within that larger system. The MC case therefore speaks to the need for greater institutional care, protection, and commitment when scaling intermediation—a lesson introduced here and further explored through the North Carolina biomanufacturing case in chapter 5.

## The Program's Foundations

Manufacturing Connect officially started in 2005, but its institutional genesis dates back several decades and has strong links to long-standing efforts to protect manufacturing businesses and middle-class manufacturing jobs in Chicago. In 1982 the Chicago-based labor activist and former manufacturing worker Dan Swinney created an advocacy nonprofit to conduct applied research on the city's urban manufacturing job loss. Swinney and his collaborators gathered real-time information at the establishment and

neighborhood level in an attempt to influence corporate relocation decisions. They joined other organizations as part of a larger, city-funded initiative
called the Local Industrial Retention Initiative, or LIRI, that was spearheaded
by Chicago's mayor at the time, Harold Washington.[6] LIRI initially served as
an "early warning" system for potential plant closings and relocations.[7] The
initiative relied on a delegation of community-based organizations throughout Chicago that built relationships with the small factories and used those
exchanges to identify the root causes of their economic distress.

As with others involved in the LIRI network, Swinney initially set his
sights on locally rooted manufacturing companies that were threatening to
close down or relocate facilities from Chicago to low-wage countries in Latin
America. Swinney's efforts to keep established manufacturers anchored in
place garnered strong support from Chicago-based plant managers, who
equally struggled to convince high-level decision-makers, including foreign
owners of US branch plants, to retain a US manufacturing presence.

While these targeted research campaigns were not always successful in
reversing top-level relocation decisions, Swinney's tireless focus on manufacturing retention elevated his visibility within Chicago's worker advocacy
and manufacturing industry networks. In 2001 he partnered with the Chicago Labor Federation to produce a joint publication that proposed the
creation of a citywide manufacturing career pathway system. Swinney
eventually secured support from other sympathetic partners to form an
umbrella organization in 2005, and founded the Chicago Manufacturing
Renaissance Council (CMRC). This unique coalition, with representatives
from organized labor, manufacturing firms, local government, community
leaders, and educational institutions, is still active today and continues to
promote Chicago manufacturing as a catalyst for "building a society that is
economically, socially and environmentally sustainable and restorative."[8]

Like Swinney, other early members of the CMRC recognized that urban
manufacturing job losses were not inevitable but resulted from specific,
localized constraints, such as industrial land conversion or endemic institutional gaps—challenges that could be addressed through community
action. One of the CMRC's earliest objectives was the creation of a new
educational infrastructure to support "a consistent stream of educated and
skilled young people to provide leadership in all aspects of manufacturing."[9]
As part of that effort, the council initiated plans in the mid-2000s to establish a manufacturing-oriented high school, recognizing that manufacturing

industry upgrading had to be paired with concurrent investments in workforce education and training.

The CMRC selected the Austin community for this new high school initiative, with the goal of bringing large-scale economic opportunity to an impoverished West Side neighborhood. Austin was (and remains) a predominantly African American neighborhood, with approximately one quarter of all households, and nearly 40 percent of households with children, living below the federal poverty line. But this high-poverty neighborhood also has a long manufacturing history, and CMRC saw an opportunity to reengage this industrial legacy and leverage manufacturing activities in surrounding Chicago neighborhoods. As Swinney explained, "Rebuilding manufacturing in Chicago should begin in those communities hit the hardest by deindustrialization like Austin. We [the CMRC] believe that these communities need to be prioritized in promoting development despite the many difficulties."[10]

The CMRC worked closely with leaders from CPS to open the Austin Polytechnic Academy in 2006 as a traditional public high school. CMRC pushed this public school format because of its long-standing commitment to job quality standards: as a public high school, Austin teachers would be covered by a union contract with quality wages and benefits protected under a collective bargaining agreement. The school, which eventually changed its name to the Austin College and Career Academy (ACCA), draws the majority of its students from the surrounding Austin neighborhood. Representative of neighborhood demographics, the vast majority of ACCA students are African American, and most reside in low-income households.

### Real-World Learning

Up until its late 2019 departure from the ACCA, the MC program functioned as an optional elective available to all enrolled students. Each year, up to 65 percent of ACCA students participated in MC's program. Since graduating its first cohort in 2011, MC has supported more than two hundred ACCA students. In 2017 the program was replicated in two other Chicago public high schools, Bowen and Prosser, adding additional students to the MC roster.

MC was launched concurrently with the ACCA as a set of manufacturing and applied engineering electives and related work-based learning opportunities. These elective courses and applied learning opportunities started in students' sophomore year. They were tied to industry-recognized credentials, with "stackable" modules that were certified through the National Institute for Metalworking Skills (NIMS), a metalworking trade association established in 1995 to develop and maintain an American manufacturing workforce. The Manufacturing Renaissance Council chose to align the school with NIMS because of the portable nature of these credentials, as well as the institute's occupational reach and strong industry support. NIMS certification is valued not just by Chicago-based employers but has nationwide credibility. MC participants at the ACCA had the opportunity to earn up to five NIMS credentials, the most popular being Materials, Measurements and Safety and Computer Numerical Control Turning Operator. Between 2011 and 2018, 189 MC students received at least one NIMS credential, and most earned two or more by the time they graduated.

Though the MC program was an elective, it was not kept separate from the rest of the ACCA community or curriculum. During their time at the ACCA, MC staff worked closely with the school's instructional core to incorporate manufacturing and engineering concepts into daily lesson plans. One example is an ACCA geometry class that my research assistant, Julie Stern, observed in 2016. During the class period, students were exposed to core engineering concepts through an applied activity that asked them to determine wingspan-to-length-to-seating ratios of different aircraft models. For this particular class, representatives from aerospace giant Boeing Corporation were on-site to assist. The reverse situation was just as common: academic knowledge from nonelective science and math classes frequently made its way into MC's manufacturing coursework. The goal was to use this curriculum alignment to reinforce classroom learning through a real-world application—which, as MC program director Erica Staley emphasized in one of our discussions, meant designing MC's engineering and manufacturing electives to make math and other high school subjects "come alive."

As a public high school–based program, it should come as no surprise that reinforcing classroom education has been a top priority for MC. But students engaged in the MC program also benefited from soft skill and leadership training, the latter designed to entice them to consider management and ownership roles as possibilities in their careers. Student leadership was further developed through extracurricular activities, best exemplified by MECH Creations, a student-run cooperative that was created in 2013 to produce custom trumpet mouthpieces, launched with product design input from an MC machining instructor and jazz trumpeter.

With this additional leadership and business development training, the MC program prepared students to succeed at all levels of the firm. As Dan Swinney notes, "We regularly have to clarify that ACCA is not a trade or vocational school but one geared to all careers related to manufacturing, including all positions within the firm as well as positions outside the firm. Our career range includes skilled production technicians, marketing and management, ownership, a Ph.D. researcher in nanotechnology, or a leader in industrial policy."[11] The program strived to show students that there was value in training for diverse positions along the entire manufacturing career spectrum. Reflecting this, one student in a promotional video for the school noted, "My long-term goal is ... to own my own company that gives back to the community."[12]

An added layer of student support came in the form of individualized college counseling. From day one, MC staff worked alongside counselors at the ACCA, advising students with strong interests in engineering or related fields on which college programs to apply for in order to round out existing academic and technical interests. Over the years, MC has formalized its own programming in support of college enrollment and reported these results along with other metrics it uses to measure student and program achievement. Among MC's senior class of 2018, 100 percent of students applied to and were accepted by at least one college, and one-third of the cohort received a formal scholarship offer; crucially, the entire 2018 graduating class had submitted a FAFSA application, thereby increasing their chances of securing financial aid.

As a result of this support, the majority of MC students have opted to enroll in a college degree program immediately following their high school graduation. Within each graduating cohort, roughly two-thirds have enrolled in college, with 40 percent entering a two-year associate's degree program and 60 percent starting a four-year bachelor's degree program. MC leaders and staff have widely publicized and celebrated this achievement, noting that some of these college-bound students have pursued engineering degrees that will support manufacturing industry innovation in the years to come.

But college is not the only postgraduation route that MC has actively promoted to its students. MC teachers and administrators have helped graduates who chose not to enroll in college determine their next career step. They have helped these students recognize the value of pursuing immediate work while also keeping open the option for higher education. One former student we interviewed from the 2012 cohort who chose to accept a manufacturing job acknowledged that he anticipated enrolling in a college degree program at some point in the future. He also stressed that participation in the MC program helped him recognize the importance of placing his postgraduation decision within a larger career context, including exploring options for employer-sponsored tuition reimbursement. Another former student admitted delaying the college decision in order to support other family members; in this particular case, accepting a secure job now with good salary support and benefits enabled the individual to accumulate savings, which could be tapped later to lower college debt levels for self and their younger siblings.

As these examples suggest, MC students were not pushed to seek a college degree for its own sake, nor did they approach that decision lightly or in haste. Rather, their experience with MC encouraged them to consider multiple opportunities and objectives, including the value of paid work in extending career choices and economic mobility to other family members. In this regard, MC's impact is not limited to individual program participants but spills over into the wider Austin community, just as its founders envisioned.

### Employer Engagement

With its combination of applied coursework, college advising, leadership training, and industry-recognized technical credentials, MC has helped public school students in the high-poverty Austin neighborhood gain foundational knowledge to embark on rewarding manufacturing careers after graduation. But to complete the translation of student learning objectives and career preparation into quality job opportunities—especially for students who seek employment immediately after high school graduation—MC also recognized a need to work from the other direction, from employer to worker. In other words, it had to act as an intermediary, engaging employers in ways that shifted their perceptions of inner-city youth and helped them recognize the contributions of younger workers for firm survival and industry innovation.

How has MC achieved this? And how has it navigated the unique challenges of working with employers to advocate for young, first-time job seekers?

Like other intermediaries mentioned in this book, MC brings about changes to established hiring and training practices through ongoing employer engagement—work that MC continues today even as it restructures in its new home outside the public school system. When physically located within the ACCA, staff at MC started this process by engaging small and medium-sized manufacturers in close proximity to the high school, encouraging them to become active "partners" in the program. Between 2011 and 2018, MC engaged well over a hundred small and medium-sized manufacturing firms, though admittedly a much smaller group of around thirty core partners remained actively involved in supporting the program over multiple consecutive years.

At a basic level, MC solicited input from its manufacturing partners on curriculum development, with a subset of firms invited to formally advise them on the right mix of equipment and machinery to include within ACCA classrooms, including the machine shop. Interestingly, as a result of manufacturer input, MC determined early on that it was best to fill the school's machine shop with equipment that most closely resembled what students would experience as entry-level manufacturing workers. Over the years, this meant intentionally avoiding technology upgrades that might be considered too sophisticated given student knowledge, or whose use in a firm was likely restricted to more experienced workers. The value of this decision was reinforced by a Chicago-based workforce specialist affiliated with MC and its parent organization, the Manufacturing Renaissance Council. In his words, "Just because you come in with your driver's license doesn't mean I'm going to give you the keys to the Ferrari." Employer input into technology selection and requests by MC for equipment donations ensured a close match between the classroom learning environment and what ACCA students would first experience on the shop floor; it helped set realistic expectations and establish common ground.

Beyond advising on technology selection, MC also called on its partner manufacturing firms to assess the quality of student work. This included incorporating employers into the NIMS certification process at ACCA. In cases that involved a more advanced NIMS credential, for example, a student would start with a blueprint of an object, convert it to a computer image, and then make each component using classroom machining equipment. The student would then complete a competency-based test to demonstrate proper use of a particular machine, technique, or skill set. A partner company's role was to independently assess the part to determine whether it met precise specifications. Once the company approved the part, the student would advance to the final online examination.

As Erica Staley notes, this competency-based testing was "not about seat time, or 'OK, you've taken X hours, therefore you must know something by now.'" Rather, for MC students, it captured applied learning while also instilling an appreciation for quality standards and accountability to a client or employer. For partner employers, it gave them an opportunity to observe ACCA students in a serious learning environment. By involving employers in this review, MC was able to reinforce industry buy-in for NIMS certification, which in turn sent a powerful message to students that this skill assessment process was worthwhile and highly valued.

Admittedly, student assessments and curriculum reviews were relatively low-effort activities for partner firms; they did not require much in terms of time and resources. In this respect, these partner-engaging activities were not so different from what one might expect to find at more traditional technical education programs. But MC took things to the next level, using these small requests as starting points when engaging a new or prospective partner firm. In other words, once an employer indicated support for the ACCA-based program, it was encouraged to commit to more intensive commitments in support of student learning.

At a minimum, partners were asked to sponsor a class tour or invite a student or two to complete a one-day job shadow of an existing employee. This gave students a more realistic understanding of what a modern-day manufacturing facility looks like, with the option to visit multiple factories to compare different work environments. Partners were also called on to support short-term paid internships, either when MC students were on summer break from school or during shorter school vacations such as spring break. In addition, partner firms provided work-study opportunities to more senior students, including paid after-school employment for students nearing graduation.

Between 2011 and 2018, employer partners sponsored close to five hundred work-based learning experiences, often combining these options so that students moved through a reinforcing sequence from factory tour to work-study placement to summer internship. These exchanges were designed to "build cultural bridges" between students and manufacturing firms. For students, this meant an opportunity to move through multiple manufacturing firms, gaining a deeper appreciation for organizational nuance, yet also observing and comparing different occupational pathways. For the employers, it was a way to follow student processes and growth over time and come to appreciate the role of MC in providing students with foundational technical knowledge and soft skill development.

It is here, in its concurrent work supporting student interns and their sponsoring firms, that MC solidified its role as a workforce intermediary. By working bidirectionally, preparing students for work while encouraging firms to engage with young job seekers, MC improved the school-to-work transition and helped employers extend opportunities for skill development and career advancement to newer employees, particularly youth with limited prior work experience.

## Entrenched Hiring Practices as Barriers to Youth Employment

Before examining MC's employer-facing strategies in greater detail, it is useful to first understand the hiring and employment practices that partner firms often started out with and reflect on how they might undermine youth job retention and career development, even for those students that completed a successful internship.[13] As noted earlier, the majority of MC's employer partners are small and medium-sized manufacturing businesses; this was also the case for the subset of firms they actively worked with during their time at ACCA. The median size of an MC partner firm is around forty employees, with its largest partner a notable outlier with around eight hundred workers. Most of these partners manufacture metal products or parts, ranging from springs and gears to large finished goods such as industrial ovens, transit seating, and high-end airbrushes. Many of these firms are family-owned businesses, and most have an aging, primarily White workforce that is fast approaching retirement.

Our research team conducted open-ended interviews with company owners and plant managers from 2015 to 2017. From these discussions, we learned that prior to their involvement in MC, partner firms tended to hire workers informally, through social networks or by word-of-mouth. This included asking their existing workforce to recommend friends and family members. One employer, with an average worker tenure of nearly thirty years, shared an example of his preferred hiring strategy by pointing to a current employee whose mother had worked there well before she was born; now mother and daughter work together at the factory.

The practice of hiring through personal networks meant these partners emphasized social connections and firm loyalty over skills and experience. As one employer said, "We've had a pretty low bar as far as qualifications are concerned," which in that particular case given a high share of Latino immigrant workers, meant little more than a "reasonable command of the English language." While a few employers favored applicants with a formal industry credential, they were not particular as to type, treating it less as proof of technical skill and more as an indicator of general interest in manufacturing.

The tendency of these employers to hire on the basis of social ties over specific skills or educational preparation presented both an opportunity and a challenge for a workforce intermediary like MC. It implied some degree of flexibility around hiring, as employer partners were willing to take a chance on any job seeker who came recommended by a trusted source. At the same time, it created an invisible barrier for those lacking the right social connections or who were unable to decode what the firm required or desired from a new employee to gain a foothold in the company.

Employers also acknowledged that this informality around hiring carried over to worker advancement. Admittedly, many MC partner firms entered the ACCA-based program with some elements of a structured career ladder already in place, including differentiated shop floor job functions that progressed with skill. Workers at these firms could, in theory, move up these implicit ladders: each firm we interviewed offered concrete examples of top-level supervisors who had progressed through the ranks starting from entry-level positions. Several even emphasized that, given a choice, they much preferred to "grow their own" talent than fill those positions through external recruitment.

Still, few firms entered the MC partnership with consistent policies around advancement, and most lacked clear communication channels for sharing information about new job openings with eligible workers. In some cases, worker advancement was also based on manager identification of desirable characteristics, but these qualities were entirely subjective or not closely tied to demonstrated technical competency. For example, one employer said the most important quality it looked for in a job applicant was "follow-up," meaning "simply doing what you say you're going to do and communicating that well with supervisors and co-workers." The interlocutor went on to stress that "people that are responsible enough to do that … are the ones that are going to make it." Another employer said that workers that had advanced in his firm often shared an innate "curiosity" and a desire for continued learning about manufacturing, though those qualities were not well defined.

And even in cases where advancement opportunities were available, more often than not, the onus was on the employee to make their interest known to management. As one employer stressed, "If someone has interest, they could go to the plant manager, they could go to HR and say, 'I'm a machine operator, I'd like to learn more skills.' ... And we won't say no." While on the surface this attitude seems inclusive, practices like this could be a major deterrent to workers who are reticent to self-advocate and put themselves forward as a potential candidate. For others, there might be an additional barrier if they lacked awareness of the unwritten expectation that the worker should initiate the process.

When pushed further on the subject, one employer acknowledged that communication gaps around advancement had long existed at his firm. As he put it, "We recognize that some people view their positions as dead ends, and it doesn't have to be that way, if the person is willing to progressively work at it—and we want those people to do that." But, as he admitted, "We don't do a great job of communicating that, but that's what we want." Another owner of a manufacturing company mentioned that supervisors and plant managers had often failed to adequately mentor less senior workers, meaning it was hard to "pluck these people out." In these cases, the problem was not a lack of desire on the part of the employer to advance their workers; rather, what was often missing was a formal and consistent structure for making the policy known to all workers, especially those new to the firm.

Another common missing piece at MC partner firms was an explicit training protocol that workers could shape into a rewarding internal career ladder. Although many MC firms had previously offered employees some form of on-the-job training, skill development tended to be haphazard, lacking the cohesive framework necessary for generating long-term value for employees. Training typically took the form of a short-term fix, mostly occurring on an as-needed or even emergency basis.

Production demands often reinforced a focus on "spot training" rather than longer-term career planning. One employer, when asked to reflect on the connection between production and training, explained: "I certainly understand that they feed off each other and it gets into a positive cycle, so that if we had a formal program in place with more training, that's going to make our workers more productive and that's going to make everything go upward." Still, he also recognized an underlying friction with this dynamic, noting that it is "easier said than done. In the short run, ... we've got a day-to-day business to run and satisfying our customers is number one." By extension, deeper investments in training were seen as a distraction.

Given this challenge and others, some firms chose to participate in the MC program out of a desire to strengthen their internal workforce infrastructure—and they noted that their involvement in the program only reinforced their awareness of that need. Many also joined the program to broaden their options for new worker recruitment. Reinforcing this view, some firm owners admitted it was becoming increasingly difficult to rely on "friends and family" hiring sources, especially with younger relatives of current employees growing less interested in manufacturing careers.

Manufacturing Connect was created to give firms an attractive alternative for reaching job seekers well beyond their existing social networks. Still, the internal challenges and tensions described in this section meant that extending a job offer to a younger job seeker was rarely enough to guarantee quality employment opportunities. Without additional improvements to internal structures and workplace dynamics, firms faced high rates of worker turnover. Cognizant of this risk, MC staff were fully prepared to help firms active in the ACCA-based program introduce real and lasting organizational changes.

### First, the Charitable Pitch

Many of the interviews cited above were with firms well entrenched in the MC program, meaning they had plenty of time—for some, as much as a decade—to reflect on and resolve internal limitations, and also to experience firsthand the benefits of their partnership with MC. But newcomers to the program often lacked that critical insight, so that MC staff had to be ready with strategies to push firms to look critically at their own internal constraints and modify workplace practices and structures to better support a younger workforce.

An initial step involved appealing to employers' intrinsic desire to be good philanthropic organizations and give back to their surrounding community. As Bill Vogel, the former partner outreach coordinator for MC, explained it, "There is something that's inherently valuable to any organization when you're helping a young person. We feel it's in our bones, it's in our DNA, to want to share our experience with a young person, hopefully that we can influence that young person's life." Reinforcing this perspective, the owner of one manufacturing partner firm noted that he initially became interested in the MC program because it was a good fit for his company's philanthropic profile—a local school, focused on education and supporting underserved Chicago youth. He also stressed the personal satisfaction he derived from his work with MC students, noting that "these kids need every advantage they could possibly get." He went on to elaborate that "as much as I'd like to see the success of Chicago Manufacturing Renaissance [an organization he also supports], I'm really focused on this community and this particular set of kids and seeing them succeed." Emphasizing a similar sense of moral obligation, another employer stated, "I'm a firm believer [that] we need to give these young people an opportunity. We have a social responsibility as manufacturers."

Over the years, MC staff have nurtured and leveraged this philanthropic commitment. Indeed, a key distinction between MC and many other workforce intermediaries is that MC staff explicitly approached employer partners and asked them for help. MC staff consistently communicated that employers were "true partners" in creating socioeconomic change and, because of that, were expected to co-invest in the program and the surrounding community, not just extract the benefits. When employers joined MC, they were expected to contribute between $500 and $750 to the program up-front. They also signed a letter of commitment promising to participate in prehiring activities such as hosting job shadows and internships, participating on advisory committees, or participating in promotional events to recruit other prospective employers.

This philanthropic hook has often led firms to initially soften their interpretation of student actions at work, and to respond to student mistakes differently from how they would have responded to the same mistakes made by more experienced workers. One MC employer partner described a situation in which a high school student, recruited through a different program, was caught stealing lunches during a summer internship placement. Through his involvement with MC, this employer knew of the tremendous challenges that poverty creates for low-income students. In response to the theft, the employer opted not to dismiss the student outright. Rather, he used the incident as a conversational moment to uncover the underlying circumstances that might have led the student to act in this way. Through discussion, it became clear the theft stemmed from a lack of money and limited food options at home, which in turn resulted in further action by the employer to subsidize lunch and provide other supports.

Similarly, another employer noted initial concern on discovering that summer interns from MC had not deposited their paychecks many days after receiving them. In speaking with the students, the employer learned they did not have their own bank accounts or proper identification. The employer responded by taking the students to the Social Security office and then to a local bank branch so they could create individual saving accounts and build a financial history. In yet another example, an MC summer intern arrived at work wearing baggy jeans that sat low on his hips, reflecting a long-popular fashion trend for young men. With a broader social mission in mind, this employer took time to explain in detail why this attire was unsafe given the surrounding manufacturing equipment and described clothing more appropriate to this particular work setting and other professional environments. Importantly, the employer was sympathetic and nonjudgmental in that exchange. They chalked the intern's garb up to "normal kid things" and even compared his choice to differing views over acceptable hair length they had once encountered when they were young and new to manufacturing employment.

Reinforcing as much, another employer indicated that, as a result of MC's primary mission to improve socioeconomic outcomes for low-income students, it "[did not] expect Austin [MC] to tailor a program for us." This was different from the employer's expectations of other training programs, which it instead categorized as instrumental to the company's bottom line and improved performance. In contrast, the employer noted that with MC, the onus was on it, the company, to bend toward the needs of younger job seekers, even if that meant initially relaxing certain standards.

These examples are among many others that MC partner employers shared with us to illustrate the benefits for younger, less experienced job seekers when potential employers interpret their behavior through a philanthropic filter. Owners and supervisors were more sympathetic and less likely to turn immediately to punitive steps when something went wrong. They were willing to forgive an initial misstep and take time to remedy the situation by fostering open dialogue and building a common understanding with young workers.

Still, reliance on the charitable leanings of company executives has its limits, especially if that is the *only* strategy in play for employer engagement. Accommodation of certain actions by younger workers can quickly sour, particularly if the same behavior is not tolerated from the permanent workforce. Also, if students are not given a chance to learn expected workplace practices, they do not benefit from an opportunity to display that learning and maturity to coworkers.

Because of this downside, some US labor scholars have advised school-to-work programs like MC to avoid this charitable approach entirely, not just because it muddies workplace rules and norms but because it can undermine youth career development by encouraging employers to view their role narrowly as a form of social welfare.[14] But this recommendation assumes that this "feel-good" strategy is enacted in isolation, which is not the case with MC. Rather, its strategy was to build *from* that philanthropic drive, leveraging that initial community commitment as the foundation from which to push partner employers to embrace even greater procedural and structural changes.

## Institutionalizing Internal Change

While MC staff used their multiple interactions with partner employers to translate initial goodwill into meaningful employment opportunities, the longer internship period (lasting upward of three months) proved especially helpful in bringing to light problems within a company that required improvements to entrenched HR practices. Several employers we interviewed described feeling woefully "underprepared" when hosting their first cohort of summer or spring break MC interns. They subsequently requested additional help from MC staff to improve their ability to give students a more successful initial work experience. One employer, reflecting on early exchanges with Austin students, stressed that "the bottom line is that we need to be prepared just as much as the students are when they come in to work."

MC staff maintained an ongoing practice of frequent visits to partner employers during the internship period, often dropping by unannounced to solicit real-time input on the process. MC also used information gathered during these informal exchanges to make improvements to its own pre-internship curriculum and related classroom activities to prepare students for an initial work placement. Still, as much as these exchanges helped create stronger relationships between MC staff and employers, they also pushed employers to rethink established human resource practices. For employers, these exchanges helped reinforce a sense of shared responsibility for educating younger workers.

After discussing a difficult first internship experience with MC staff, one company owner realized the need to initiate a series of conversations with shop floor supervisors to improve things for the next round of interns. "I talked to one of my top manufacturing guys. I said, 'Look, we're bringing a kid or two in here over the summer and I really need it to work. The last [students] floundered a bit because they didn't have a mentor to help them out. They need guidance.'" The owner went on to stress, "There was sort of an 'Aha!' moment with the manufacturing guy [and] he says, 'You didn't tell me that's what you wanted!' So he thought about it and said, 'I have some ideas and now I'm going to nurture and make sure these guys [from MC] have a better experience when they come through here.'"

In this particular example, the primary challenge was a communication gap between executive leadership and shop floor supervisors—the latter assigned responsibility for the day-to-day management of student interns. Simply through improved communication, company leaders were able to impress on shop floor supervisors the need to implement strategies that would improve the internship experience of future MC students.

Employer partners also used the internship experience and internship-related meetings with MC staff to engage supervisors in conversations about the need to build a more transparent and robust workforce pipeline. One employer, for example, initiated conversations with incumbent shop floor supervisors about the learning expectations of MC interns and stressed during these exchanges that some of the students could become the supervisors' mentees or coworkers in the future. The employer also emphasized that in supporting these younger job seekers, the supervisors were contributing to the lasting legacy of the firm and Chicago's manufacturing industry.

Still, motivational messages from company owners were not always sufficient to resolve the deeper frictions that emerged when employers brought MC graduates on as full-time employees. Multiple partner firms described incumbent workers resenting the advancement of an MC graduate, in some cases viewing it as a form of preferential treatment. One employer emphasized this point by describing a situation in which an MC graduate they had hired was marked for advancement by upper management but whose direct supervisor was "giving him a hard time ... because he sees this kid has a lot of attention on him." While the firm's owner communicated new expectations to supervisors, they failed to recognize the dissonance this created with established organizational practices and routines. As such, supervisors initially perceived the MC graduate as receiving much better treatment compared to what they themselves had experienced earlier in their careers.

Another firm owner indicated that their incumbent workforce was initially fearful that newly hired MC graduates were being trained to replace them at lower levels of pay.

Ultimately, resolving tensions like these required substantial changes to workplace practices and routines. While change is difficult to manage, as is any major cultural shift in a workplace, initial disharmony created an opportunity for MC staff to work more closely with employers to help identify deeper structural changes that would benefit younger workers, including MC graduates—and that could also help improve the overall work environment for older, incumbent employees. MC staff used frequent visits with employer partners and weekly debriefing sessions with student interns to draw out these frictions, then approached employers with a range of options for how to mitigate conflict, typically starting with better work structures and routines. Additionally, MC convened workshops with employer partners, sometimes structuring those events as peer learning sessions at which firm owners could share advice and suggestions with each other.

Drawing on this peer support, one partner employer was able to take steps to formalize internal mentoring strategies, not only as a means to better communicate expectations to newly hired MC graduates but also to empower the incumbent workforce. This intervention was in response to a situation described in the opening vignettes in this chapter in which an MC graduate introduced an innovative but unauthorized change to an established shop floor process without first seeking authorization from his assigned supervisor. Rather than engaging the student directly and thus circumventing established chains of command within the firm, the firm's owner approached the incumbent foreman and empowered that person to use the opportunity to develop a better approach for new employee training and supervision. The employer realized that "someone needs to tell them [the MC graduates] before it [the mistake] happens." The foreman was able to review standard operating practices with the MC graduate, yet also emphasize the value of maintaining open communication and dialogue to ensure workforce cohesion. By granting authority to the foreman, the firm owner was not attempting to reinforce power structures or knowledge asymmetries. Rather, the goal was to bring two generations of workers together and build a more trusting shop floor relationship—one that would also inspire midlevel supervisors to develop applied learning opportunities to encourage younger workers to creatively problem solve.

Reiterating this point, a MC staff member noted: "We have to educate our [partner] companies with a lot of older workers, on how to even deal with the youth. ... Don't put them in a role where they are just going to clean. They're going to get bored. You're going to get mad, and then end up firing them. Give them something meaningful to do, otherwise they are going to discredit this whole program. ... They want to be interested, they want to be engaged. They want you to speak to them, they want you to talk to them." And stressing that with pending worker retirements, younger workers represented the future of manufacturing, she added the message that the older generation must "adapt."

One employer noted the same, observing that as a result of MC-inspired improvements to employee mentoring, more senior supervisors became proactive in preparing for young workers to enter the organization, even taking the initiative to independently develop work-based learning opportunities for a cohort of four MC graduates the firm had hired in 2016. This company also relied on input from supervisors and MC staff to design a new system for all entry-level employee training. Based on that feedback, the company added an official "buddy" system whereby new employees were paired with one or two existing workers who could help them navigate the new work environment. Newly hired workers, including MC graduates, had a say in this matchmaking process, including exercising the option to request a buddy reassignment. By allowing this change to be driven by a new worker, the company created a system for aligning more compatible workers and personality types. As the company's HR manager also noted, "We try and get different perspectives because somebody can think, 'Oh, [the new worker] is not getting it, and they're not going to make it.' But then someone else [in our company] may see something else in that person." By triangulating information, the employer not only avoided making biased decisions on the basis of narrow or subjective input, it reduced the risk that younger workers would feel vulnerable within this new work environment.

In consultation with MC staff, this same firm recently took additional steps to establish a more transparent protocol for "onboarding" younger interns and better preparing them to meet the expectations of daily work life. As an example, student interns, along with their assigned supervisor, were asked to sign a formal contract that clearly outlined company expectations and explained the consequences students would face for violating the terms of that agreement; the contract included specifying the number of warnings student interns would receive before a notice of final termination. As emphasized by the company's HR manager, "I think it's our responsibility in working with Manufacturing Connect to tell [students] 'Nope, it's not acceptable. I'm not going to terminate you, I'm not going to fire you, but at the same time I need to tell [you] that this is unacceptable, and you need to correct this behavior.'" MC staff worked with other partners to adopt a similar process, including encouraging the use of an explicit "three strikes and you're out" termination policy. By making this process transparent, companies ensured all students learned workplace rules their first day at work while also creating a clear enforcement structure designed to protect their well-being and economic future as they transitioned to permanent employment.

Other notable structural changes stemmed from continued employer engagement by MC staff, which widened opportunities for workforce intermediation. One employer acknowledged drawing inspiration from his continued experience hiring MC graduates to introduce company-wide strategies for better integration of *all* new employees. As a result of his MC experience, he learned to be especially sensitive to potential frictions between his existing workforce and newly hired "skilled" (as opposed to entry-level) workers. This helped him respond when tensions arose after he hired highly trained welders, who were able to demand significantly higher starting wages than his incumbent workforce did. This wage difference was mostly due to differences in qualifications, including knowledge of specialized welding techniques. Nonetheless, the conflict this pay differential created made it much harder for his company to retain newly hired welders, especially in the context of high regional demand for certified welders.

To solve this problem, the employer drew on his long-standing connection to MC to get help in developing an in-house welding apprenticeship program to equalize skills and pay scales across the company's incumbent and newly hired workforce. As apprenticeship was beyond MC's expertise, MC encouraged the company to engage another regional workforce intermediary in Chicago. While the resulting apprenticeship program was not designed specifically with MC graduates in mind, this example nonetheless demonstrates the ways in which initial changes introduced in support of MC students are inspiring partner employers to identify and resolve broader HR bottlenecks within their organizations. Furthermore, this presents a critical opportunity for MC to build on employers' willingness to extend special consideration and treatment to MC graduates, initially for philanthropic reasons, leveraging that openness into a commitment to improve and institutionalize workforce practices more broadly.

## Parting Lessons

In a program aimed at helping economically vulnerable youth, it would be easy to fall back on a more standard educational routine and assume that any problems related to job access and career advancement will be resolved if the students first enter college and complete their degree. That assumption, which has long dominated public discourse, has intensified in recent decades as prominent foundations, including the Gates and Lumina Foundations, have spent hundreds of millions of dollars to increase college enrollment and completion rates. But with college enrollment rates now plateaued, due in large part to the added challenge of skyrocketing student debt, there is growing awareness of the need to think beyond the "college for all" mantra and broaden the options for youth to secure skills and advance their career prospects.

The MC case demonstrates that successful labor market interventions in support of younger, disadvantaged populations require a joint focus on educational opportunities *and* employer transformation. Classroom training, including focused periods of work-based learning, has served an important function in generating manufacturing employment opportunities for each graduating cohort of MC. Still, as we see from this case, employers have also needed to commit to transforming that initial work experience into a lasting career opportunity.

MC motivated firms to make this commitment with two interconnected principles: giving disadvantaged youth a helping hand *and* turning a critical gaze inward to initiate youth-supporting organizational transformation within the firm. During its time embedded in the ACCA, MC played a critical role in helping firms recognize a strong connection between these two objectives. Underscoring the program's philanthropic commitment, MC staff pushed firms to create openings for disadvantaged youth in Chicago's Austin neighborhood. Yet early mismatches between students' expectations and firms' existing workforce practices allowed MC staff to convince employers to institute new structures and routines. Under the umbrella of practicing philanthropy, it became easier for firms to admit ways their existing practices fell short, thus fostering experimentation with mentoring, supervision, and new employee training. When strategies specifically in support of MC students began to cause friction in the broader workforce, MC staff then encouraged firms to leverage their investment in the program to adopt more widespread organizational changes.

Perhaps the most significant transformation to firms' HR strategies has been at the meta level: as employers have recognized the need to improve their internal workforce infrastructure, they have returned to MC and other Chicago-based workforce providers to secure additional support in making firm-level changes. As firms continue to deepen their commitment to institutional change, they embrace MC's originating goal, positioning themselves as true partners in the transformation of Chicago's manufacturing industry. Ultimately, this helps shift some of the economic burden from educational institutions to the surrounding business community, encouraging the latter to become a catalyst for industrial transformation while nurturing an upcoming generation of manufacturing workers.

MC has clearly made progress on the intermediary front, engaging employers in novel ways and enabling them to recognize the importance of their contributions to industry workforce development. As of August 2019, ninety of the more than three hundred students who had graduated from the MC program had secured permanent postgraduation employment in manufacturing in the Greater Chicago area. Of these, well over half had surpassed the program's 365-day job retention target. The average starting wage of MC graduates as of August 2019 was around $15/hour, and one former MC student was earning $70,000 annually within a few years of graduation.

Although only a quarter of all MC students moved into manufacturing careers following graduation, growing numbers have reconnected with MC a few years after high school to get further help in securing manufacturing-related work. To encourage more connections like this, MC continues to provide program graduates with job placement and mentorship services on an open-ended basis. Additional assistance is available through an MC-sponsored peer support initiative called the Young Manufacturing Association, which hosts monthly meetings and networking events to connect MC graduates and other young manufacturing workers in the Chicagoland area. And MC staff remain active in supporting successful relationships between former students and employers after students have joined the manufacturing workforce—helping workers and employers continue to navigate and resolve tensions as they arise. Ultimately, this continued support means that placement numbers for recently graduated MC classes are likely to rise in coming years.

Of course, the MC experiment is not without its limits. Leaders in the organization have been forthcoming about the numerous challenges they encountered in their first decade, starting with the choice to simultaneously launch a public high school, which generated a unique set of organizational problems. They are also acutely aware of the need to forge partnerships with other kinds of manufacturing support institutions, including manufacturing extension experts in the Greater Chicago area. The prospects for this kind of alliance were discussed at the end of chapter 3, and in the case of MC would allow them to address production bottlenecks that can limit deeper investments by partner employers in workforce development.

Furthermore, there remain open questions about how the MC program will be structured and funded in the future. These uncertainties were brought into stark relief with MC's unexpected expulsion from its three high school homes in November 2019. A lapse in top-down communication about changing lease requirements for third-party vendors led the school district to ask MC to suddenly leave all three schools at once—but, knowing the value of the program, the district gave MC the option to participate in an open bidding process to secure a new contract, which, if awarded, would allow them back into schools. But even with its fate unknown, MC was using the time to reflect on its original organizational model. MC leaders turned to partner employers for guidance and support, asking important questions about Manufacturing Connect 2.0: Should MC remain an embedded in-school program, or would it be better to reemerge as an independent training facility with greater flexibility to serve disadvantaged students across the entire Chicago region? Should MC position itself as an external thought partner for other school districts, helping the state of Illinois extend work-based learning opportunities, including youth apprenticeship? And if this is the route taken, how can MC mitigate fears that youth apprenticeship opportunities would serve only a subset of more privileged youngsters? Should MC expand its services to include more teacher training, leveraging its long-standing relationship with the city's teachers labor union, thus building a network of champions to drive continued change within schools?

Regardless of which direction MC takes, the organization's leaders hope that its decade-long connection to Chicago's public high schools will have a lasting institutional effect on the larger Chicago Public School system. As that system decides how best to fill the gap left in the wake of MC's premature departure, it too must be willing to adapt and change, learning to appreciate the complexity of steps needed to transform places of work to foster youth employment success. For this to occur, the public education system might even consider taking up the role of an intermediary, stepping in to leverage growing interest in industry-recognized skills to acquire "soft power" to influence job access and workplace skill development through its engagement with local employers—a new and important institutional role for public educators and one that is taken up in the next chapter.

# 5 Reinterpretation Writ Large

In the late 1990s, Biogen, a high-growth biotechnology startup based in Cambridge, Massachusetts, opted to relax educational requirements for production positions at its biomanufacturing facility in Durham, North Carolina. This change opened quality job opportunities for individuals with transferable manufacturing experience yet who possessed little more than a high school degree. Reinforcing this decision, Biogen partnered with educators and bioscience workforce specialists to prototype a series of short training modules for production workers, which would eventually become a semester-long community college certificate program with a nearly universal template for hiring criteria for biomanufacturers throughout the state. A decade later, Biogen selected this same Durham-based facility—now nine hundred employees strong—as its global testing site for increasing throughput and incorporating flexible systems and disposable technologies in support of small-batch production. Those changes, which involved a two-year strategic planning process and accompanying investments of over $70 million, set the standard for process and technological improvements at other Biogen production facilities in Europe and North America. Individuals overseeing the North Carolina project have noted the essential contribution of shop floor worker input for identifying and solving production bottlenecks in published accounts about this award-winning, state-of-the art upgrade. To harness that "grassroots knowledge," supervisors in charge of the North Carolina project spent weeks embedded in the production workforce. They then worked with plant managers to create more permanent systems for engaging production workers and soliciting their input on cost- and time-saving measures. The structures they put in place ensured production workers would be recognized and rewarded through higher pay for their skills contribution, often independent of formal education.

A few years later, Eisai, another biopharmaceutical firm with large-scale production facilities in Durham—this one with Japanese roots—rolled out its own ambitious restructuring plan in anticipation of several blockbuster therapeutics moving off patent protection. Unlike Biogen, Eisai anticipated there would unfortunately be accompanying cuts to employment, potentially affecting up to 25 percent of the company's North Carolina workforce. Rather than rushing to initiate these layoffs, which would have entailed hundreds of production workers abruptly losing well-paying, family-sustaining jobs and employment benefits, Eisai chose instead to adopt an incremental approach, relying initially on normal attrition and the retirement of older workers to trim employment. But the company went a step further, transferring some of its production capacity to Biogen through a ten-year lease agreement covering a section of Eisai's Durham-based production facility and corresponding production lines. In the process, the two companies worked out a unique labor-sharing arrangement, transitioning a portion of Eisai's incumbent workforce with expertise in injectable solution manufacturing (e.g., vaccines and other liquid therapeutics) to Biogen, thereby granting fifty production workers continued job security in biomanufacturing. Eisai then concentrated its remaining resources on improving its solid-dose tableting (pill-making) division, and, in anticipation of future industry demand for third-party contract manufacturing, extended a mix of formal and on-the-job training opportunities to incumbent workers, few of whom held college degrees, in its packaging and logistics divisions, enabling them to advance into more lucrative positions in drug manufacturing.

Further afield, in Winston-Salem, North Carolina, Herbalife, a prominent natural products manufacturer, launched an extensive new employee training program to coincide with its January 2015 opening of a state-of-the art, 800,000-square-foot manufacturing plant. To staff up this new production facility, Herbalife scheduled worker training sessions at a neighboring community college, which it augmented through in-house "toolbox training" sessions and related on-the-job mentoring. Like Biogen and Eisai, Herbalife continues to invest heavily in workforce training, offering incumbent workers opportunities to expand their technical knowledge and creating personalized training plans that not only align with individual career interests but also encourage cross-task learning in support of on-site troubleshooting, problem solving, and job rotation. According to the company's industrial training supervisor, Patrick O'Sullivan, training investments of this type "build morale with the person … build self-esteem" and provide the added benefit of reducing turnover—a point he strongly emphasized, noting that "investing in people keeps them here—without a doubt."[1]

These three firms display a number of common characteristics, ones also shared with other firms in North Carolina's biopharmaceutical, natural product, and food-related manufacturing industries. These are prominent multi-site or multinational corporations that established major production facilities in North Carolina as part of a strategy to expand their national manufacturing footprint—or, in the case of foreign-owned firms, out of a desire to increase their visibility and standing within the US health care or nutritional product market. Additionally, these firms have robust internal human resource programs, with staff capacity to manage sophisticated in-house training systems and support individualized professional and career development planning for employees, including the front-line production workforce.

But a third shared feature is most noteworthy. These opening vignettes are not simply illustrations that larger, better-resourced, and more enlightened corporations are capable of supporting job quality and career development—something we might expect from these multinationals in advanced manufacturing. They are visible signs of an ongoing, evolving relationship between these firms and a far-reaching network of state-funded community colleges in North Carolina, educational institutions that provide industry-recognized training and skill development support to hundreds of firms in North Carolina's biopharmaceutical industry and related industries. In essence, the employment practices outlined above—and particularly the fact that they are structured to be inclusive of and beneficial to workers without a college degree—are a testament to the tremendous influence the state's community college system has over industry hiring, promotion, and training decisions.

In other states, jobs in the biopharmaceutical industry are disproportionally filled by workers with bachelor's degrees or higher, regardless of whether the position is production or research-based. Not so in North Carolina, which boasts the most inclusive employment profile of all leading US biopharmaceutical states: job seekers with lower levels of formal education have equitable access to quality job opportunities and the gains in economic mobility that those jobs create.

This result is not an accident, nor is it a necessary if less-than-ideal accommodation of lower educational attainment rates. Rather, hiring inclusive of those at the lower end of the educational spectrum reflects an intentional decision by community colleges in North Carolina to enact intermediary strategies similar to those described earlier in this book, namely, to use their institutional position to pull in job seekers who might have transferable experiences and insights to share, even if those qualities are not reflected in higher formal education.

But there are also important differences in how skill-focused intermediation plays out when publicly funded community colleges are at the helm. These colleges are situated within a well-funded state educational system, and from that position of influence they are able to effect change across an entire sector rather than limiting their sway to industry margins, as other intermediaries have had to do. Their expansive statewide geographic reach also sets them apart from other programs featured in this book. Those earlier described efforts, while extremely effective, are often "hyperlocal," working within a specific urban area or subindustry context. By contrast, intermediary colleges in North Carolina are touching firms and workers in multiple counties and jurisdictions. They do this by engaging larger, more prominent firms and using state support for customized training to establish high-profile relationships that help magnify their industry influence and extend their geographic reach.

This chapter explores what intermediation looks like when educational and workforce practitioners cast a wider, more expansive industry and spatial net in their quest to reshape education and employment opportunities for the most vulnerable workers. But it also considers the challenges that come with this institutional undertaking. In many respects, targeting larger firms and reaching a large number of them is a more challenging workforce proposition than focusing on smaller, resource-constrained firms, especially as the organizational vulnerabilities of the latter are more obvious and thus can be more easily leveraged to negotiate changes to entrenched practices and routines. Not only are larger firms more complex entities characterized by nested levels of decision-making authority, they are more likely to have sophisticated HR management systems for recruiting new employees and promoting incumbent workers from within, and thus have better-calibrated hiring preferences and procedures. This not only makes it harder for mediating colleges to determine when and where to insert themselves but also suggests the need for coordinated strategies of employer engagement to sustain institutional involvement and influence.

What might negotiations around skill look like within a larger organizational and farther-reaching institutional context? How can mediating institutions gain influence over the hiring, promotion, and training decisions of larger firms, with the goal of increasing or sustaining access to quality employment opportunities for less educated individuals throughout an industry? Finally, how can intermediaries maintain their industry command over skill preferences and practices, especially during periods of heightened economic or even political uncertainty?

Much like their nonprofit counterparts, mentioned in chapters 4 and 5, that work with smaller manufacturers in midwestern states, the community colleges at the center of this case have gained industry influence by "following the pain,"[2] recognizing that larger manufacturers also face intermittent workforce challenges that open channels for institutional intervention. Still, these community colleges do not just step aside once that pain subsides. Rather, they maintain their industry influence and relevance by being part of a larger integrating institutional platform that enables them to identify new targets for workforce development and worker advocacy.

In featuring the North Carolina case, this chapter showcases a potentially replicable model for embedding nested strategies of workforce intermediation within state-funded economic and workforce development systems. In contrast to the Manufacturing Connect case described in chapter 4, these intermediaries *are* the public educational system, rather than independent nonprofit, nongovernmental partners. But this case also points to emerging economic and political challenges that can affect public sector intermediation, including new pressure points that require large-scale strategy adaptation. For large public institutions facing the dual mandate of serving students and industry, institutional retreat is not an option. Instead, these community colleges must devise innovative strategies to keep working on intermediary goals even during protracted periods of industry downturn. Recent economic and political shifts in the state of North Carolina provide an illustration of what this institutional response looks like, in turn suggesting transferable lessons for how other regions might use their own community college systems to scale up and sustain intermediation in uncertain economic times.

## Scaling through System

Community colleges are the fundamental building blocks of North Carolina's contemporary bioscience workforce infrastructure and thus an essential focal point for understanding how workforce intermediaries implement and adapt strategies of skill reinterpretation. North Carolina has an extensive yet decentralized community college system, with fifty-eight community college campuses located throughout the state. The system was initially established in 1957 and grew rapidly until adding its fifty-eighth campus in 1978; its growth was enabled by strong approval and financial backing from the state's General Assembly. Individual colleges within this state-funded system have long supported workforce development in the biosciences and pharmaceuticals. Prior to the late 1990s, colleges mostly acted as training brokers, helping biopharmaceutical and related chemical manufacturers gain access to or assess fee-based services offered by "freelance" or third-party training experts both within and outside the state. Community colleges also helped these firms secure state and federal workforce development funding to offset the cost of firm-specific investments in customized training.

Over the past two decades, community colleges in North Carolina have increased their direct involvement in biopharmaceutical workforce development, and in the process, some have found ways to also become stronger advocates for less educated job seekers and workers. Today, community colleges throughout the state offer a range of open enrollment programs in biopharmaceutical science and manufacturing. Offerings include prehire, entry-level nondegree credentials and related short courses lasting a week to a semester; two-year associate's degrees in applied biotechnology; and structured articulation programs between community colleges that help a student transition from community college to a four-year university. Community colleges in North Carolina also provide customized training services, giving firms the option to offer workforce training either on a college campus or at their own jobsite. Today, approximately one quarter of North Carolina's fifty-eight community colleges provide some form of workforce training or educational programming in support of pharmaceuticals and biomanufacturing—and in most cases, the colleges that do so are physically located within counties or regions of the state that are also home to well-established or fast-growing clusters of bioscience and related firms. In addition, two community colleges, Forsyth Technical Community College and

Alamance Community College, are leading nationwide initiatives to develop industry-recognized biopharmaceutical skill assessments and certifications.

While the specific menu of training and educational supports in bio-pharmaceuticals can vary greatly from one college to the next, it is important to recognize that no institution is developing its bioscience programming in isolation. These colleges are supported through a sector-specific training and educational consortium called NCBioImpact, which helps community college–based administrators and instructors gain access to other sector institutions and biopharmaceutical employers throughout North Carolina. Through exchanges with industry experts and employer firms, including biopharmaceutical manufacturers newly recruited to the state, NCBio-Impact's participating colleges are able to anticipate new and emerging workforce challenges and identify opportunities for further institutional intervention and coordination.

This coordinated approach to bioscience workforce development has a deep history. It started twenty years ago with an initial inquiry from Novo-zymes, a foreign-owned enzyme manufacturer with a large-scale produc-tion facility in Franklin County, North Carolina. In 1998, HR managers at Novozymes approached administrators at neighboring Vance-Granville Com-munity College with a novel proposition: to codevelop a training program in support of on-the-job learning for new and incumbent workers.[3] At the time, Novozymes was in the early stages of incorporating biologic-based manufacturing processes to boost enzyme production. The company recog-nized the need for structured training to upskill its incumbent workforce, but also wanted to expedite facility expansion by hiring new production operators and quality control experts with foundational knowledge of biotechnology. With limited in-house biotechnology expertise, Vance-Granville Community College reached out to the North Carolina Biotechnology Center (Biotech Center), a nonprofit organization created in 1981 by North Carolina's state legislature as the first state-funded bioscience economic development agency in the United States.[4]

Ultimately, the Biotech Center's involvement meant this company-college partnership would result in much more than a one-off training solution for Novozymes. Biotech Center staff recognized this collaboration as an oppor-tunity to create a multiuse training program that would support expansion and hiring at multiple biopharmaceutical manufacturing facilities around the state, and in turn create a means to retrain unemployed workers from declining manufacturing sectors in North Carolina. And it also helped that education was already a top priority for the Biotech Center, which had the internal resources to dedicate to curriculum development and diffusion.

The Biotech Center had launched its own internal educational support program back in the mid-1980s. Initially, the center treated education as public outreach, supporting K–12 programming that would help increase public interest in and consumer awareness of biotechnology by educating North Carolinian youth of the benefits of biotechnology with the hope they would become informed bioscience ambassadors who could help assuage public fears of "genetic engineering."[5] Starting in 1986, the Education and Training Program (eventually renamed the Education and Training Division) upped its educational commitment and began offering competitive grants to educators in primary and secondary schools and colleges and universities throughout the state. Funding from the program helped launch numerous initiatives designed to raise interest in science careers among North Carolinian youth. As Steven Burke, an early Biotech Center executive explained, "Our assumption was that long-term positioning of anything [biotech-related] in society really starts very young in the educational system." The division also created fellowships and workshops to support professional development for high school and middle school science teachers, and funding streams for schools to upgrade laboratory equipment and classroom supplies.[6]

In January 2005 the Biotech Center's Education and Training Division had a sizable staff, an annual working budget of close to half a million dollars, and additional resources for grant and workshop support. Within the Biotech Center's organizational structure, it was positioned on an equal footing with two other divisions—Science and Technology Development, with its main focus on developing university and institutional research capabilities, and Business and Technology Development, oriented toward commercializing technologies, including supporting new entrepreneurial ventures. The Biotech Center treated these three divisions as a holy trinity of sorts—each was eventually assigned an executive vice president—reinforcing the assumption that concurrent support for public and higher education, institutional capacity building, and technological and entrepreneurial development were necessary for an emerging technology to take root and flourish in society.

But the initial training inquiry from Vance-Granville Community College in 1998 did not just resonate with the Biotech Center's core educational mission. The college's request for help also surfaced at a pivotal moment for the state's bioscience industry. At issue was increased industry frustration over North Carolina's tightening urban labor market and the difficulties this created for retaining an educated biopharmaceutical workforce. HR managers at large biopharmaceutical production facilities noted especially the footloose nature of college-educated workers, particularly those with bachelor's degrees or higher. While recent graduates of North Carolina universities applied in droves for entry-level manufacturing jobs in biopharmaceuticals, they typically did so to gain access to the state's fast-growing bioscience industry; a limited number of bachelor's degree holders had interest in staying put as front-line production workers. At the time, opportunities for mobility for university-educated job seekers were plentiful, including internal options within firms to secure better-paying positions in quality assurance, research and development, or operations management. Additional labor market tightening came from active "poaching" of employees by other life science manufacturing operations, luring employees to cutting-edge work at innovative biotechnology startups that offered exciting, fast-paced alternatives, often within more intimate yet dynamic entrepreneurial settings. Job opportunities at "homegrown" bioscience startups proved especially attractive to younger North Carolinians fresh out of university science programs, some tempted by employee stock options that came with the prospect of a lucrative payout from a high-profile exit or initial public offering. By the late 1990s, most large-scale biopharmaceutical manufacturers in North Carolina were struggling with rising worker turnover, and, not surprisingly, they turned to the state's well-positioned Biotechnology Center for help.

Vance-Granville's request for help provided the necessary catalyst for the Biotech Center's Education and Training Division to move beyond its traditional role as an external funder of existing educational programs and initiatives. Novozymes' need for upskilling allowed staff at the Biotech Center to roll up their shirtsleeves and develop the prototype for, and eventually launch, a brand-new statewide curriculum in support of biomanufacturing workforce development. In doing so, the center sought not just a training solution for Novozymes; it also had in mind the nagging turnover challenge affecting multiple biomanufacturers in the state, especially those in more densely populated metropolitan regions, where worker poaching was most pronounced. One plant manager at a midsized biomanufacturing firm in the Research Triangle region of the state acknowledged that during the 1990s, there was a lot of "trading" back and forth of employees, and while "the risk in small biotech (was) much greater ... [for some] the reward might be considered much greater as well." But, he also stressed, "We didn't want to be just trading people, we wanted to grow the workforce in the area here." This deepening labor market challenge threatened to stall growth in North Carolina's burgeoning biomanufacturing industry and thus was of uppermost concern for the Biotech Center.

The staff of the Education and Training Division of the Biotech Center were well aware of the problems and costs associated with increased worker turnover and recognized the need to develop an effective long-term solution. This and related employment concerns were openly discussed at industry events and gatherings in the latter half of the 1990s. These conversations inspired the center to create a series of industry surveys to help quantify the extent of this and other workforce challenges. In early 2000s, the center published its initial survey results in a report titled *Window on the Workplace*; it would go on to conduct additional surveys and update this publication within a few years. Around that time, the Education and Training Division was also involved in a new working group called the Biomanufacturing and Pharmaceutical Training Consortium, which held monthly meetings at the Biotech Center. Encouraged by leaders from a newly created industry association, NCBio, the center pushed for this Biomanufacturing and Pharmaceutical Training Consortium to have broad representation from educational institutions and industry (including HR professionals and plant managers) in the hope that doing so would encourage better alignment of state training resources and industry workforce needs.

If it had been left entirely to industry to solve, this intensifying workforce problem might simply have resulted in increased pressure on North Carolina's universities to boost enrollment rates in bioscience-related bachelor's degree programs. But with the Biotech Center at the helm, a different institutional solution was devised, one with longlasting implications for job access and inclusion. Dr. Kathleen Kennedy, then vice president of the center's Education and Training Division, was quick to recognize that this acute workforce challenge presented an opportunity to convince biomanufacturing firms to soften their educational requirements and expand the pool of eligible job candidates to include those with little to no college education. And Dr. Kennedy and her Biotech Center colleagues had a particular target population of qualified candidates in mind: recently displaced workers who had lost jobs in North Carolina's traditional manufacturing industries, especially furniture, tobacco processing, and textiles, which together had shed more than 100,000 jobs in the decade between 1990 and 2000.

It might seem antiquated, even retrogressive, for an economic development organization established with the express purpose of promoting economic opportunity through the development of a then novel and cutting-edge technology to push for widespread hiring of a less educated, traditional industry workforce. But this "boundary-spanning" move reflected a broader strategy long embraced by the Biotech Center: intentionally connecting biotechnology to existing industries in the state. As an illustration, the center's first published annual report in 1986 featured a memorable cover image that visually captured the contribution of biotechnology to legacy industries throughout North Carolina. The cover depicted a research scientist in a white coat, a herd of pigs at his side, and in the background a lush forest of native longleaf pine trees. This choice for the report's glossy cover was both symbolic and deliberate. It was meant to demystify a then unknown technology while also sending a powerful message to politicians (especially those from rural counties of the state) that biotechnology was an enabling technology with the potential to extend, not upend, economic opportunity for North Carolina's legacy industries and their talented and dedicated labor force.

The Biotech Center's decision to use its support for training and education to open employment opportunities in biomanufacturing for displaced manufacturing workers was well within its core mission. With traditional industries such as textiles and tobacco processing in an employment freefall, policymakers in North Carolina were desperately looking for employment alternatives—well-paying, family-sustaining jobs for a skilled yet less educated manufacturing workforce. The Biotech Center recognized the transferability of the skills of this legacy workforce and was prepared to do its part to promote such a transition. Still, Biotech Center staff also realized that it would not be enough simply to espouse the benefits of hiring less educated workers with prior manufacturing experience, perhaps by emphasizing their loyalty, appreciation, or staying power. Rather, they needed to create an adaptive training tool to facilitate workforce transition and career mobility, one that would establish foundational knowledge in core areas of biopharmaceutical manufacturing and resolve employer fears that hiring workers with lower levels of formal education might compromise product or process quality.

Novozymes' desire to work with Vance-Granville Community College on a structured worker retraining program provided an ideal test case. At the time of the program's inception in the late 1990s, few existing production workers at the Franklinton-based facility had more than a high school degree, a situation that presented a unique opportunity to prototype elements of a rigorous and inclusive retraining program. Noting this, Novozymes agreed to pretest early versions of the new training modules and instructional materials on its incumbent workforce. Eventually, Novozymes would take the next step, interviewing job applicants who had completed the first semester of an open enrollment version of the course at Vance-Granville in 2001. Feedback on those applicants resulted in yet another round of revisions to the original training prototype, including the addition of job placement modules on résumé writing and interview preparation.

In the meantime, the Biotech Center also invited other biopharmaceutical firms to weigh in on the program. Another half-dozen firms were asked to test-run training modules and materials on their existing workforce and provide feedback on curriculum design. The Biotech Center used a mix of complementary methods to compile and compare information on different production systems and training needs, identifying areas of overlap and distinction. Over the course of many months, staff from the Biotech Center toured dozens of facilities around the state, meeting extensively with HR and plant managers in the process. They also shadowed production workers and plant supervisors to observe firsthand the manufacturing process and determine how best to codify aspects for the purposes of classroom instruction. These exchanges were not just used by center staff to forge deeper connections within industry, they also facilitated a "paradigm shift of sorts," enabling the center to push back against entrenched propriety norms by showing which aspects of manufacturing operations were standardized across multiple biopharmaceutical companies and thus good candidates for training coordination.[7]

In addition to Novozymes, the Biotech Center convinced the company Biogen to be an early partner in testing an industry-wide, multisite curriculum. The Massachusetts-based biotechnology firm selected North Carolina in the mid-1990s for a large-scale manufacturing facility to produce Avonex, a human therapeutic used in the treatment of multiple sclerosis—a location decision that was aided by a Duke University alumni connection. As with many high-profile corporate recruitment deals in North Carolina, Biogen received a commitment from the state government to assist with new employee recruitment and training—a forward-looking if nonconformist strategy, insofar as most neighboring southern states were dangling offers of cash incentives but with little regard for workforce training, at least at that time. Coming from a state with exceptional educational offerings, Biogen was especially pleased with North Carolina's commitment to workforce development. In anticipation of hiring, HR managers at the firm worked closely with training experts from the Biotech Center and community college system to further modify the Vance-Granville curriculum to meet its own employment needs.

Merck Manufacturing, Leiner Health Products, Eon Labs, and Purdue Pharmaceuticals also provided input on the proposed training curriculum. At the time, these firms had large-scale facilities in Wilson County, North Carolina, but used traditional, chemical-based rather than biologics-based production methods to manufacture human therapeutics. While biologics are produced using some form of recombinant DNA process, also known as biotechnology, chemical-based pharmaceuticals require some combination of different chemical ingredients, and therefore the production steps for the two are quite different.

Because of the proximity of these four firms, the Biotech Center solicited help from instructors at Wilson Technical Community College to develop a set of alternative training modules in chemical mixing, solid-dose tableting, and coating, in addition to the cell growth and culturing modules in development at Vance-Granville. Wilson Tech's involvement added flexibility to the core curriculum, ensuring it could be easily adapted to support training needs at other chemical-based pharmaceutical manufacturing facilities throughout the state.

The vocational training program that was created through this multiyear, multifacility exchange still exists today. Called BioWork, it remains a minimum hiring requirement for many pharmaceutical-related firms in North Carolina. Twelve community colleges in the state, starting with Vance-Granville, added the BioWork program to their course catalog between 2001 and 2006. In 2005, approximately nine hundred individuals completed the

BioWork program in open-enrollment sessions (as opposed to customized versions for a particular firm). While annual enrollment has fluctuated, including a dip in the wake of the Great Recession, BioWork annual completion rates still averaged around 740 individuals per year from 2008 to 2014.

Today's BioWork course is an updated version of the original and reflects further input from industry experts. Still, BioWork remains a 128-hour, semester-long certificate course that focuses on entry-level process technician skills for both biomanufacturing and chemical-based pharmaceutical manufacturing. Enrollment in BioWork requires only a high school degree or GED equivalent; additional remediation options in math and reading are supported through a pre-BioWork feeder course, free to qualified applicants. BioWork's nine training modules focus on a range of topics, from safety and quality control to process sterilization and the growth of living cells. Companies throughout the state are also given the option to customize the BioWork program, mixing and matching modules as needed to support incumbent worker training.

### Multilevel Intermediation

While BioWork and related certificate courses in biopharmaceuticals have benefited from Biotech Center staff involvement, it is ultimately the responsibility of the trainers and administrators at individual community colleges to deliver this course and customize versions of it for firms within their assigned jurisdiction. This blurring of boundaries between industry training needs and publicly funded community colleges might lead some to question the ability of public educators to effectively balance the needs of workers and students, both present and future, with those of prominent employers in their region. But in North Carolina, individual community colleges have used their close ties to both the Biotech Center and biopharmaceutical employers to double down on efforts to influence industry hiring practices and preferences in ways that are inclusive of less educated job seekers in their region. In this respect, workforce intermediation is not only visible in the actions taken by leaders and staff at the Biotech Center, it is also enacted at the community college level.

I had a chance to first observe the contribution of college-level workforce intermediation in 2006, when my UNC colleagues and I conducted surveys of students enrolled in the BioWork program.[8] At the time, only seven community colleges in North Carolina offered regularly scheduled, general-enrollment BioWork courses. And while each remained faithful to the original curriculum, they differed tremendously in their capacity to move beyond classroom instruction to also influence employer decision-making. In 2006, we categorized four of the seven colleges as "strong mediating institutions," meaning they leveraged ongoing relationships with bioscience employers in their service catchment area to facilitate and shape local hiring to the benefit of workers with fewer educational or economic advantages; the remaining three were categorized as having weak or nonexistent intermediary strategies. Each of the four "strong" colleges had either worked closely with Biotech Center staff in developing the original BioWork program or had benefited from a high concentration of biopharmaceutical manufacturing facilities in their respective region, allowing opportunities to hone strategies of employer engagement. The four standouts in the mid-2000s were Johnston Community College, Wake Technical Community College, Wilson Technical Community College, and Vance-Granville Community College—all based in counties within or in close proximity to the Research Triangle region of North Carolina. Other colleges, including Durham Tech, have since joined their ranks.[9]

The strong intermediary colleges each employed a variety of strategies to shape local hiring decisions in biopharmaceuticals. At a minimum, training and administrative staff from these four colleges were in regular contact with supervisors and HR managers at bioscience companies in their service area. In some cases, this was done by scheduling frequent face-to-face meetings with representatives from individual companies; in other cases, it involved weekly or bimonthly phone conversations. These exchanges served two purposes. First, they allowed college staff to closely follow industry trends and their potential effect on local employment, including anticipated establishment-level job openings or layoffs. Second, they provided a direct communication channel for identifying new opportunities for worker training that could be addressed through additional college intervention and support. Discussions with workforce practitioners indicate these community colleges continue to use these employer engagement strategies today.

Intermediary colleges also hired additional or specialized staff to facilitate employer engagement. Johnston Community College, for example, hired a part-time job counselor with bioscience industry experience whose primary role was to conduct outreach at local biopharmaceutical facilities.

This counselor also worked closely with BioWork students who were seeking jobs in the biosciences. By embedding herself further within local employer networks, she was able to strengthen her position as both jobs broker and student advocate. Similarly, at Vance-Granville Community College, a Bio-Work instructor was hired directly from Novozymes, which at the time was the largest bioprocessing facility in the college's assigned jurisdiction. This instructor was also able to draw on her existing connections with company personnel to establish and maintain a close working relationship between the company and the college. At these and other intermediary colleges, a good number of BioWork instructors maintained full-time employment at local bioscience firms. These individuals were contracted by the colleges as part-time instructors, receiving permission from their employers to do so, with the goal of sharing industry insight and knowledge with BioWork students.

Intermediary colleges often drew on these same employer networks when designing and equipping physical classroom spaces and soliciting equipment donations from bioscience companies. At Johnston Community College, for example, classroom laboratories used for BioWork training were named after the county's large-scale bioprocessing firms at the time, including NovoNordisk, Hospira, and Talecris. These named labs not only contained equipment donated by these and other companies, they were located in a satellite training facility on land deeded to the college by these same companies. These companies were also asked to contribute financially to a college training fund, which helped defray the operating costs of the satellite facility. The training center continues to offer open-enrollment BioWork courses for prospective bioscience job seekers today; in fact, Johnston Community College has the highest BioWork annual completion rate of any North Carolina college, averaging well over five hundred completions per year. The training center also continues to train incumbent bioscience workers during regularly scheduled maintenance shutdowns. In neighboring Wilson County, Wilson Tech Community College also established close ties with local bioscience employers. Because most pharmaceutical firms in Wilson Tech's service area rely on chemical rather than biological production processes, Wilson Tech was motivated to work closely with these firms to modify BioWork course modules to ensure the content was technologically relevant.

How, then, did these four intermediary colleges use their relationships with bioscience employers to influence local hiring—that is, to mediate the relationship between job seeker and local employer? At a basic level, all four intermediary colleges used these connections to give students opportunities to meet with prominent staff and managers at local bioscience firms. Intermediary colleges often organized tours at large bioscience facilities in their service areas to allow BioWork students to observe the specific work environments they were preparing to enter. They also invited HR personnel and manufacturing supervisors from the facilities into the BioWork classrooms to discuss employment-related issues and concerns, including advising students on interviewing and résumé development. Johnston Community College formalized this approach by initiating a speaker series in the mid-2000s with invited representatives from different companies in its service area. BioWork students from the college were encouraged to attend these sessions and were given an opportunity to network with company representatives.

But these colleges pushed further to influence local hiring. Wilson Tech Community College provides an illustrative example. As noted earlier, the college helped training experts at the Biotech Center modify the original BioWork curriculum to meet the needs of chemical-based pharmaceutical firms. In exchange for accommodating those needs, college administrators at Wilson Tech convinced pharmaceutical manufacturers in the region to guarantee job interviews for the college's recent BioWork graduates. This arrangement not only gave graduates of the Wilson Tech program a leg up in the application process, it also allowed college administrators to request timely feedback from these companies when Wilson applicants were not offered a job. Other intermediaries also built on their close relationships with local employers to actively promote their BioWork graduates. Vance-Granville, for example, provided Novozymes with lists of top-performing students from each BioWork cohort. Students on that list then received a Novozymes job application, which HR managers kept on file until a job opening became available. As with the arrangement established by Wilson College, this list-sharing functioned as a de facto "first-source" referral arrangement, giving students from these colleges early advantages in their job search. Although Wilson Tech and Vance-Granville went the farthest to formalize these arrangements, Johnston and Wake Tech Community Colleges also used their strong relationships with local bioscience employers to extend their labor market influence. Instructors at both colleges frequently provided references for short-listed candidates in their respective programs. They also reached deep into their networks of BioWork and other community college alumni to help graduates of their programs secure interviews at local bioscience firms.

## Does College Intermediation Matter?

In 2005, I had an opportunity to work with an exceptional team of UNC–Chapel Hill graduate students, along with my UNC mentor at the time, Harvey Goldstein, to test whether these intermediary practices had a significant effect on bioscience employment in North Carolina. For this research project, our team surveyed students who were enrolled in the semester-long Bio-Work certificate program at seven community colleges, and used the results of those surveys to determine whether or not students at the four strong intermediary colleges had a better chance of securing job offers in biomanufacturing. With this research, we did not focus on subsequent organizational changes within companies but rather on that first critical step in workforce intermediation, shaping hiring decisions, as this step influences who gains access to quality job opportunities in larger biomanufacturing facilities that already offer robust internal career ladders for entry-level workers.

With this cross-college comparison, we were able to factor in the intensity of intermediation at the college level and capture its subsequent effect on employment outcomes. Because we also used our surveys to collect demographic details for each student, including information about the individual's educational and employment experience that pointed to potential barriers to employment, we were able to test whether those barriers were reduced for students who were enrolled at a strong intermediary college. Put simply, did their employment prospects improve because their college had developed close relationships with employers? Were those connections effective in helping students get a leg up in the hiring process, especially students with gaps in education or experience that might otherwise result in their application landing in the reject pile?

As we discovered, demographic characteristics (race, ethnicity and gender) were not strong predictors of whether or not applicants received a job offer. Nor did overall education matter much, with the important exception of college-level coursework in science or math, which did strengthen employment results a bit. Overall, job seekers with previous employment in some form of advanced manufacturing, especially microprocessing, performed even better—which made sense because of the overlapping manufacturing processes, including shared (and regulated) production standards, commonly referred to as "good manufacturing practices," or GMP. Biopharmaceutical employers clearly recognized some added value in harnessing this transferable experience, knowing the microprocessing workforce was also expected to follow strict product quality requirements.

But our key finding was that college-level intermediation mattered most. Students enrolled at one of the four strong intermediary community colleges had a significantly higher chance of receiving a bioscience job offer, even if they had less formal education or accumulated work experience than other applicants. Strong intermediary colleges were able to close the job-offer gap between those with college and work experience and those without: all students at intermediary schools had a strong fighting chance at securing an industry job, thanks to the ongoing connections these colleges had with area employers. And that inclusive employment outcome reinforces the point that public educational systems can position themselves as effective and influential intermediaries. Our research demonstrates that community colleges can use their ongoing relationships with employer firms to shape local hiring decisions, and in doing so level the playing field for students who might otherwise have a harder time securing a quality job. Workforce intermediation is possible not just through building stronger institutional partnerships between nonprofits and public education systems. The public sector can also be responsible for intermediation, helping the employers they support through industry-recognized credentials also rethink their hiring and skill needs.

## How Does North Carolina Compare?

More than a decade has passed since my colleagues and I conducted our initial study of the effects of community college–level intermediation on bioscience employment in North Carolina. Much has changed since 2006, not only for North Carolina but for our nation as well. The intervening period has been punctuated by the 2008–2009 Great Recession, which hit North Carolina as hard as other southern states, with North Carolina experiencing especially large job losses in manufacturing. The political environment in North Carolina has also changed considerably, with the Republican Party seizing control of both houses of the state legislature in the 2010 election. This raises some obvious questions: Are community colleges in North Carolina still able

to command labor market influence in the state's biopharmaceutical industry today? Have they modified their strategies over the years, and if so, in
what ways and in response to what kinds of economic or political pressures
or opportunities?

To address these questions, it is useful to first outline several broad trends
with respect to biopharmaceutical manufacturing employment, not just for
North Carolina but for all US states with similar industry profiles. For this,
I draw on a more recent cross-state comparison that I conducted with my
collaborator, Laura Wolf-Powers, to illustrate the influence that workforce
intermediation has had on North Carolina's unique bioscience employment profile.[10]

Nationwide, the US bioscience industry employs approximately 1.5 million workers in more than 77,000 business establishments.[11] Bioscience
establishments in North Carolina employ around 70,000 workers, and that
number is growing. Between 2001 and 2014, North Carolina experienced
40 percent employment growth in this industry, and continued to add jobs
during and immediately after the Great Recession—a time of considerable
economic volatility when most other leading bioscience states were experiencing sizable employment declines. In fact, between 2009 and 2012, North
Carolina experienced higher bioscience employment growth than eight of
nine other leading bioscience states, with the important exception of California, with which it kept steady pace. That said, from 2012 to 2014, life
science employment growth in North Carolina topped 6 percent, compared
to 2.3 percent in California.[12] Over the past decade and a half, North Carolina's bioscience employment growth has significantly outpaced employment
gains for all private industry in the state by a ratio of 30 to 1. As emphasized
in a 2014 bioscience industry report published by Battelle Technology Partnership, "The broader economic importance of the life science industry for
North Carolina is revealed in that increases in life science industry jobs in
North Carolina stood at 48 percent of all net new jobs generated in North
Carolina over the last twelve years."[13]

Like most other leading US bioscience states, North Carolina special-
izes in certain subareas of bioscience. The state has an especially high concentration of employment in drug and pharmaceutical manufacturing,
the category that encompasses biomanufacturing. In 2012 this subarea
accounted for 20,949 jobs, or roughly 35 percent of North Carolina's overall direct bioscience employment, making North Carolina about 2.5 times

more concentrated in drug and pharmaceutical manufacturing than the national average. North Carolina also enjoys relative employment strengths in research, testing, and medical-related laboratory analysis, another bioscience subarea that generates close to 20,000 jobs in the state. While North Carolina is not as specialized in research-related activities when compared with drug and pharmaceutical manufacturing—its research-related concentration is lower, at 1.4 times the national average—it has seen sizable employment gains (8 percent) in this subarea since 2009, suggesting a move toward further specialization.

In some respects, North Carolina's concurrent strengths in bioscience production and research resonates with an existing argument that there are inherent complementarities between these two elements of biosciences that lead to and reinforce coexistence within the same region or state. Management scholars from Harvard University have argued that certain advanced manufacturing industries, biosciences included, require colocation to drive and sustain growth and innovation.[14] They point especially to a subarea of bioscience that uses recombinant DNA or biotechnology to manufacture drugs and therapeutics where the final product—be it pills, vaccines, or topical compounds—is developed through processes that involve some kind of living organism or active cellular component. They argue that when drug-making involves biotechnology or large-module biologics, it is counterproductive if not impossible to geographically separate research activities from production. Instead, there is a technological interdependency whereby production processes require continuous input from and interaction with those involved in product design, which helps explain why biotechnology-focused regions often experience mutually reinforcing employment gains in *both* production and research-oriented activities.

North Carolina's bioscience industry certainly displays this reinforcing synergy, visible in its sizable and growing number of research-intensive bio-manufacturing facilities—facilities that utilize some form of biotechnology to manufacture therapeutic products. According to the North Carolina Biotechnology Center, approximately one in three bioscience manufacturing jobs in the state's Research Triangle region takes place in a biotechnology-using facility. In most cases, these facilities have sizable internal research divisions with capabilities to support and innovate in-house production.

But this is not North Carolina's only specialized strength in bioscience manufacturing, suggesting we need to look beyond claims of technological determinism and also consider ongoing efforts by economic and workforce development practitioners to support and sustain job and establishment growth across diverse industry segments.[15] In addition to biotechnology-focused firms, North Carolina is also home to a prominent group of pharmaceutical manufacturing facilities that use more traditional chemical-based production techniques, and many of these also have a strong research base either to support new product development or aimed at improving manufacturing processes. There is the clustered group of chemical-based drug manufacturers in Wilson County that was noted earlier, with related facilities dispersed throughout the state. Other firms in this category include BASF, GlaxoSmithKline, Hospira, and Merck. Furthermore, over 50 percent of these traditional drug manufacturers maintain both a manufacturing and a research presence in North Carolina. As this implies, traditional pharmaceuticals in North Carolina are not a fading technological relic destined to be replaced by more cutting-edge processes involving biologics. Nor is the state a pharmaceutical manufacturing outpost, with production hived off from more innovation-oriented, research-supported activities. Rather, traditional pharmaceuticals remain a robust industry subspecialization in North Carolina with complementary research activities in support of process and product innovation.

North Carolina's wide range of employment opportunities in both bioscience research *and* production, and also chemical-based *and* biotech manufacturing, set it apart from other peer states. In our cross-state comparison, Laura Wolf-Powers and I found distinct and contrasting patterns in other US states that demonstrated current or historical growth in the biosciences.[16] One grouping includes New York, New Jersey, and Pennsylvania, with older traditions in chemical-based pharmaceuticals. These states have all experienced significant traditional manufacturing job loss in recent decades, though admittedly, some have gained bioscience jobs in the subfield of biotechnology. For the most part, however, the job gains in biotechnology have been modest and driven by small, dedicated research establishments with limited manufacturing capacity or potential. In a second group are states such as California and Massachusetts that have no prior pharmaceutical legacy and entered bioscience in the mid-1980s with a leading focus on biotechnology and strong specialization in research and development. While these states have experienced related biomanufacturing growth, their levels of biomanufacturing employment have been significantly lower than those in bioscience design- and research-related occupations—roughly half, in fact.[17] It is therefore rare to find a combination like that observable in North Carolina, characterized by strong production job growth in both traditional pharmaceuticals and biomanufacturing, co-occurring with equally impressive employment gains in research and design.

Along with its more balanced industrial mix, we also find that North Carolina exhibits another noteworthy distinction: the Tar Heel state has done a better job than peer bioscience states in maintaining employment opportunities in biopharmaceutical manufacturing for less-educated workers. This is especially true for drug and pharmaceutical manufacturing, where approximately 40 percent of workers in North Carolina have a high school equivalency certificate or less (figure 5.1). Another 30 percent of North Carolina's biopharmaceutical workers hold bachelor's or graduate degrees, with the remaining 30 percent securing an associate degree or

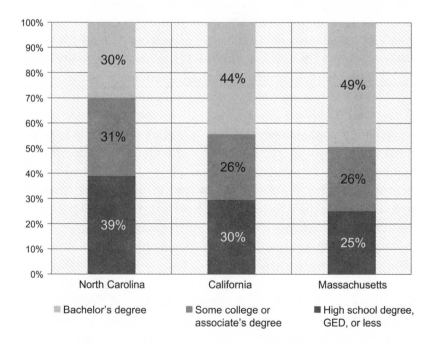

**Figure 5.1**
Pharmaceutical and drug-making industries, 2018: Share of workforce by educational attainment.
*Source:* Quarterly Workforce Indicators: Employment by educational level at all private firms. NAICS 3254. Author's analysis (data as of July 7, 2019).

some college education in support of that degree. This trend is consistent over the time period (starting in 2000) for which data are available. No other leading bioscience state has come close to achieving this educational balance. Instead, the largest share of jobs in those states goes to bioscience employees who have earned a bachelor's degree or higher.

### Emerging Economic, Political, and Technological Challenges

North Carolina's southern location might lead one to assume employment gains in the biosciences simply reflect the state's favorable taxation regime and lower labor costs. But there is a more compelling reason to consider, one tied in to North Carolina's historical commitment to promoting employment growth and skill development through institutional coordination.

With the North Carolina Biotechnology Center at the helm, the state has sustained impressive job growth across a diverse array of bioscience activities, all the while continuing to expand employment opportunities across the entire educational spectrum. Over the years, the Biotech Center has worked closely with North Carolina–based universities, creating an enviable research and educational infrastructure that attracts powerhouse multinational corporations to the state while also fostering the creation and development of "homegrown" bioscience establishments.[18] This institutional infrastructure has certainly yielded high-paying jobs for many recent university graduates, including those with advanced academic degrees in biological sciences and engineering from North Carolina's preeminent research universities. But as this chapter indicates, workforce and bioscience industry specialists in North Carolina remain committed to strategies that seek to maintain employment opportunities in biopharmaceuticals for less educated workers.

The partnership between the Biotech Center and the state's community college system is key to that continued success, with individual colleges and training centers adding further institutional depth and reinforcement. The North Carolina case shows that it is possible to use strategies of employee engagement to promote labor market inclusion, extending quality job opportunities in high-growth industries (and prominent employers within those industries) to individuals with little more than a secondary education.

Still, it would be misleading to suggest that practitioners in North Carolina have enjoyed steady, unwavering labor market influence over the

years. Complex, multilevel workforce systems like that developed to support North Carolina's bioscience industry can face intermittent operational
challenges and funding setbacks that can affect some institutional nodes
more than others, with increased risk of system fragmentation emerging
during periods of large-scale political and economic change.[19] Workforce
institutions in North Carolina are certainly not immune to economic and
political pressures, which have intensified in recent years, with all three
branches of state government ceding to Republican control in 2010 for
the first time since the post–Civil War Reconstruction period. With this in
mind, I conclude this chapter by reflecting on some of the emerging challenges this changing political environment has created for economic and
workforce practitioners.

With Republicans currently (2020) in control of the state legislature, state
funding cuts and related austerity measures are par for the course, and the Biotech Center and its affiliated training programs have not been spared. Still, in
the face of this fiscal challenge, economic development and workforce practitioners in North Carolina have experimented with novel solutions, including
making space for new industry applications and institutional coordination
and advocacy. In 2013 the Biotech Center took an especially large budget hit,
with the Republican-controlled General Assembly slashing its annual state
appropriation by 27 percent, or roughly $4.6 million. Faced with the cen-
ter's largest single-year cut in state funding since its founding in 1981, center
executives were forced to make some difficult and expedient choices. In the
end, they opted to disband entirely the Educational and Training Division
and lay off seven permanent employees in the process.

Importantly, the decision to close the Education and Training Division did
not signify diminished institutional or industry interest in workforce development. On the contrary: workforce development has remained a critical factor
in bioscience firm recruitment, retention, and expansion, a point emphasized
today by economic development professionals and executives at the center.
The division closure was instead predicated on external institutional capacity, and specifically the ability of other institutional partners—namely, those
active within the community college system—to temporarily pick up some
of the slack in the wake of deep cuts to the Biotech Center's working budget.
To facilitate this transition, the former director of the Education and Training
Division has acted in the capacity of freelance consultant, providing services

to workforce institutions that want to extend programming in support of the biosciences. Another key training specialist formerly with the Biotech Center's Education and Training Division was hired to head up professional program development at a shared learning facility (BTEC) that provides a range of educational opportunities, including weeklong intensive technical courses, to university and community college students. Staff at the Biotech Center were involved in BTEC's creation in 2007, providing workforce needs assessments and helping to write the proposal and business plan to secure $60 million for BTEC from the state's Golden Leaf Foundation.

The ability of former Biotech Center training experts to transition to new institutional roles and continue to support biomanufacturing educational programming and development in North Carolina is a testament to the continued robustness of this workforce system. It also reflects a deep determination by workforce specialists to promote institutional coordination and resilience.

Still, workforce institutions are not the only entities in North Carolina that are sharing and recycling talented workers. Bioscience firms are known to do this as well and when that happens more intensively, it can temper demand for workforce training. An example of this occurred in the immediate aftermath of the 2008–2009 Great Recession. Industry consolidation in biopharmaceuticals led several large North Carolina–based manufacturers to reduce overall employment, forcing experienced biomanufacturing workers to search for new jobs. The main beneficiaries of this industry shakeout were other North Carolina–based biopharmaceutical manufacturers that were expanding at the time, as they were able to pick up workers with tremendous industry experience—a version of what was described at the start of this chapter with Eisai's decision to downsize in the early 2000s and Biogen ready to welcome those workers. In the wake of the Great Recession, however, restructuring within biomanufacturing was more widespread, and thus the movement of workers across firms was more frequent if also less formal.

For the North Carolina community college system, the immediate effect of this workforce reshuffling was reduced demand for "new employee" training through established programs such as BioWork. Still, this slowdown did not signal the end of workforce intermediation. Instead, it motivated system adaptation. In response to uneven training needs in biopharmaceuticals, community colleges within North Carolina's BioNetwork division intensified outreach efforts to remaining biopharmaceutical firms that were poised for further growth and thus could continue to provide well-paying jobs to workers with less than a college degree. But the larger community college system also pushed further afield, recognizing the potential to redirect excess biopharmaceutical training capacity to support firms in additional industries that shared overlapping workforce profiles owing to their adherence to similar regulatory standards as biopharmaceuticals: food, beverage, and natural product manufacturing.

To facilitate wider inclusion, the system turned to knowledgeable staff at the Asheville-Buncombe Technical Community College (A-B Tech) in the western part of the state, which had already established close connections with firms in these distantly related industries. Starting in the mid-2000s, A-B Tech had partnered with natural product manufacturers in western North Carolina, adapting modules of the BioWork curriculum to fit its needs, much as its community college counterpart in Wilson County had done earlier in the decade to support chemical-based drug manufacturers. By the end of 2010, A-B Tech had further modified its BioWork training course in support of food, beverage, and dietary supplement manufacturers—all growth areas for the region, which is also recognized as a national leader in craft brewing. In 2012 the community college system formalized the BioNetwork division's expansion beyond pharmaceuticals, hiring a senior director of food, beverage, and natural products.[20]

This decision by the community college system—to build on A-B Tech's pioneering efforts—proved fortuitous in light of the 2011 US Food Safety Modernization Act, a historic and far-reaching response by federal regulators to a massive *Salmonella* outbreak in 2009 that affected close to a thousand individuals in forty-seven states. The resulting requirement for factory-wide retraining by food and beverage manufacturers throughout North Carolina was a turning point that ultimately helped BioNetwork community colleges rebound from the postrecession lull in biomanufacturing. But in casting a wider industry net, the community college system also found it could better support economic and spatial inclusion. The new industry targets it added to the BioNetwork list, especially food and beverage manufacturers, were located in more distant parts of the state, including some rural and poorer counties. By pushing beyond the state's urban core, BioNetwork has expanded the geography of opportunity, also enabling more community colleges to join the network and experiment with intermediation strategies of their own.

Non-urban manufacturers in North Carolina have especially struggled in recent years with recruiting and retaining workers. Colleges in the

BioNetwork are keenly aware of this challenge, exploring ways to push intermediation strategies even further, not only influencing who gets access to good jobs in food, beverage, and natural product manufacturing but also ensuring those jobs are also high quality and long-lasting—and therefore more in line with job quality standards in biopharmaceuticals. As the North Carolina economy continues to evolve, so too do opportunities to strengthen intermediation, with increasing numbers of colleges at the ready to help more firms throughout North Carolina become "employers of choice" by better connecting workforce training needs to *workplace* improvements.

But expanding industry influence through greater geographic reach is not the only priority for the BioNetwork division of the North Carolina community college system. This network of colleges is actively working to create improved employment opportunities for the next generation of bioscience workers, recognizing the need to embrace and facilitate technological change. Like other advanced manufacturing industries, biomanufacturers have their eye on automation, including the use of flexible production systems that combine human talent and computer-aided production processes. Rather than wait for industry to initiate these changes, BioNetwork and its affiliated community colleges are working closely with a subset of prominent employers to update training protocol, starting with the semester-long BioWork program. In early 2019, BioNetwork began testing a substantially revised version of BioWork at Johnston Community College, the influential intermediary college described above. While the original BioWork relied on cartoonlike illustrations as visual teaching aids, the updated version includes videos and online learning supports. Reflective of emerging biomanufacturing technologies, BioNetwork has also worked with industry partners to codesign a module on automated production systems, with the option to teach students through virtual reality simulations. As it strives to modernize the state's biomanufacturing curriculum and incorporate the latest technologies, BioNetwork remains faithful to a long-standing institutional tradition: engaging employers to extend opportunity to incumbent workers and job seekers across the entire educational spectrum. With this continued commitment, BioNetwork proves technological progress does not need to come at the expense of workforce inclusion, the topic examined in more detail in the next chapter.

# 6 An Inclusive Innovation Future?

Starsky Robotics is a pioneering young company, founded in 2017 in San Francisco, California. They have gone head-to-head with Tesla, Uber, and other technology giants to develop self-driving trucks, which have been tested on open roads in Florida. But their model is different from their better-known competitors, as they have put the interests of "blue-collar" workers front and center, creating "meaningful jobs" for experienced commercial truck drivers. Specifically, Starsky has worked with veteran truckers on the safe navigation of long-haul trucks through densely populated urban or industrial landscapes—what is commonly referred to in the world of autonomous vehicle development as "first and last mile" solutions.

Even the company's name symbolizes that commitment to blue-collar inclusion. "Starsky" is not simply a reference to one of the main characters in a popular 1970s television show about a Southern California cop duo—it is also a popular CB radio term for truck drivers who work in teams. Alluding to that, Starsky Robotics' model is to pair drivers with in-house robotics and artificial intelligence experts to co-develop proprietary driver-aided technology. But these teams have also informed the design of physical infrastructure, which Starsky cofounders hope will enable truck drivers in the future to remain close to their homes and families by eventually controlling fleets of vehicles from remote location work sites.

A related example is Factory OS—OS is shorthand for "off-site"—a state-of-the-art "prefab" construction facility that combines pioneering robotics technology, an in-house research and development lab, and "tried-and-true manufacturing methods to build multifamily modular buildings more efficiently and at a lower cost."[1] Factory OS is housed in a massive World War II–era ship repair and maintenance facility in Vallejo, California. And though the company has forged notable relationships with Silicon Valley investors and tech giants like Google that are desperate to house a fast-growing workforce, what really stands out is its formal connections to carpentry and building trades unions in Northern California. Factory OS collaborates with worker-supporting institutions that not only help to recruit and train the firm's workforce but are also poised to be essential partners in technological diffusion, advocating wider adoption of the firm's innovative manufactured solution to address the United States' seemingly intractable affordable housing crisis.

A third innovative company, 99Degrees Custom, is an entrepreneurial fiber technology startup based in Lawrence, Massachusetts, a city with a strong history of textile manufacturing dating back to the early nineteenth century. 99Degrees was launched in 2013 to develop and prototype innovative wearable technologies. Like its high-tech counterparts in construction and trucking, it too has adopted a worker-centered approach, hiring and cross-training experienced apparel and textiles workers from the region, turning especially to Latino and South Asian immigrant communities with legacy textile talents for help in developing high-performance, customizable fabrics and products. The company also benefits from ongoing partnerships with local universities. In 2016 it won the prestigious "Humans + Machines" grand prize from MIT, which came with a generous cash award totaling $125,000. It continues to work with university faculty and students to improve its underlying business and technology models.

Why open this final chapter with three high-tech entrepreneurial business cases, when up to now the focus of this book has been on mediating workforce institutions? My goal here is not to push business entrepreneurship as the best or only hope for expanding access to meaningful, quality jobs; technology startups, after all, are high-risk ventures, with some estimates putting the odds of failure for a new entrepreneurial venture at close to 90 percent.[2] Nor do I wish to parrot the standard innovation narrative that privileges the contribution of "risk-taking" entrepreneurial founders or their investors to new technology development, a myopic view that obscures the critical role of upfront government funding and public sector "visioning" in laying the foundations for technological progress and later-stage commercialization.[3] Reinforcing both points, as this book was nearing production in February 2020, news broke that Starsky Robotics had run out of money and would soon be folding the business—one of many promising technology start-ups to close in early 2020 in the wake of shifting invest-ment priorities.

Still, these entrepreneurial examples—whether robust or fleeting—are illustrative of something more promising. I share them because they chal-lenge contemporary mainstream thinking around automation and employ-ment, and because they highlight opportunities for institutional coordination to concurrently advance economic innovation *and* economic opportunity.[4]

Combined, these cases provide compelling evidence that leading-edge technologies can be inclusive of blue-collar front-line workers through inten-tional strategies that place less educated workers on an equal footing with highly educated technical specialists. As demonstrated by these three compa-nies, innovation does not need to be job-ending: under the right conditions, it can be opportunity-broadening. These cases—along with a growing list of others—expand what is meant by "knowledge work" and broaden our under-standing of who can lay claim to the cherished title of knowledge worker.

What these firms represent for society is a far cry from Silicon Valley's latest vision for "progressive" social policy, such as the increasingly popular idea of a universal guaranteed basic income and its close cousin, the "robot tax," both of which assume the inevitability of technological progress that destroys jobs and upends worker livelihoods. By contrast, these cases point to a very different institutional solution, with prominent research institutions and advocacy organizations stepping in, but not to clean up the employ-ment "carnage" in the wake of technological progress. In this alternative vision, their involvement helps push pioneering firms closer to an inclu-sive innovation standard, protecting job security by upholding up a shared moral sensibility to harness and promote the creative talents and contribu-tions of the front-line workforce.

How might we act on these cases and inspire others to follow their lead? For labor advocates and their academic allies who seek to support better working conditions through applied research or informed advocacy, these examples can motivate broader institutional thinking, an envisioning not just of an inclusive technological future but of a substantially different institutional landscape. To start, we should be asking more from institu-tional actors that are well poised to shape future rounds of technological innovation, holding innovation-centered institutions accountable to what Jennifer Clark aptly calls a "progressive approach to innovation policy."[5] Such institutions include federal laboratories and research universities that create the basic and applied knowledge on which novel technological applications depend, as well as government agencies and publicly funded programs that support innovation and entrepreneurship.

Expanding the reach of university-based programs like MIT's Inclusive Innovation Challenge, which financially supported 99Degrees Custom back in 2016, is an obvious first step. That program, now in its third iteration, has provided millions of dollars to more than forty companies and organizations, with close to 15 percent of awardees developing some kind of technological application that includes input from everyday workers. And opportunities to scale up that effort are not limited to research universities. The use of institutional funding to nudge more businesses to adopt inclusive innovation standards could also be incorporated into well-established programs at the federal and state levels, including the federal Small Business Innovation and Research (SBIR) grant program, which annually provides $2.5 billion to for-profit companies that employ up to five hundred workers.

But beyond additional funding support, it is also important to ask how institutions that care about the fate of less educated and vulnerable workers—including the workforce intermediaries featured in this book—can extend their influence over technology decision-making in order to promote the participation of front-line workers and protect their claims to quality jobs. In other words, how can we move workforce institutions—and by extension the vulnerable workers they seek to support—from the periphery to the forefront of innovation strategy? And related to that, how can we encourage institutions that are heavily invested in leading-edge and applied technologies to formally partner with labor advocates and workforce intermediaries?

The previous chapters of this book featured examples of workforce intermediaries engaging small and large companies around new or applied technologies. Chapter 3 discussed these intermediaries working with manufacturers on "soft" technological changes, such as transforming the organization of production to make better use of front-line workers' skills and support their career development. Chapter 4 discussed the efforts of Chicago's Manufacturing Connect to create a seamless transition from school to work by coordinating improvements to the school curriculum with training and machinery upgrades in a high school shop class and engaging a network of local manufacturing firms. This integrated approach also enables educators and workforce specialists to cross the threshold into the firm to improve on-the-job training and mentoring. Chapter 5 explored a similar case involving a coalition of North Carolina community colleges that use their relationships with firms to pull down the career ladder in biomanufacturing to less educated job seekers and provide training supports that track industry technology needs. Their efforts also undergird company initiatives to solicit input from that production workforce when introducing new equipment, engaging shop floor workers in critical decisions related to large-scale process innovation and facility-wide technology upgrades.

Importantly, these workforce intermediaries are also cognizant of their own technological limitations and the resulting need to connect with organizations that have deeper technical expertise. As noted in chapter 3, some have taken steps to formalize relationships with state or regional manufacturing extension programs, leveraging extension agents' deep knowledge of production management and engineering processes to help identify which groups of shop floor workers to engage in technology development and deployment. Other intermediaries have forged connections to sectoral economic development agencies, industry associations, university research facilities, and technology vendors, all with the goal of helping firms better align technology upgrades with workforce upskilling.

Workforce intermediaries are not blind to the ever-increasing adoption of technology and its effect on the workplace. Still, with more "radical" and profoundly transformative technological advances on the horizon, there is a need to consider what further institutional coordination or intermediation is called for. Admittedly, it is too soon to fully predict the ideal institutional mix that will be needed to support the next iteration of the American workplace. Some of it will undoubtedly depend on where technological innovation goes next; the coming decades will likely see advances in autonomous vehicle design, robotics or other applications involving artificial intelligence, machine learning, or even quantum computing. Equally, location could be a factor, especially as institutional capacity—whether on the workforce, production management, or technology front—differs substantially across state and regional lines. This geographic differential raises questions around technology policy, specifically what might be needed in the way of federal or state-level policy action to extend economic opportunity by guiding technology choices.

But even with this uncertainty, we can draw insights from both existing and historical institutional responses to new technology development that seek to place worker interests front and center. With that in mind, I have identified a half dozen cases—some current, others dating back several decades—in which institutional actors have mediated the development and deployment of emerging technologies to stabilize employment for front-line workers. Rather than describing each case independently or even chronologically, I present them in relation to cross-cutting strategies that illustrate what can be achieved through institutional intervention. Each of these strategies—admittedly at varying levels of development and geographic reach—point to an opening for contemporary workforce intermediaries to play a stronger role in rebalancing the workforce effect of new technology deployment with skill as a catalyst for employer engagement.

## A New Bargain for New Technology

As a starting place, let us consider the role labor unions play in moderating technological change. Labor unions have long intervened to ensure employers recognize and value worker skill. And that role extends to skill in the context of technology development—not only with respect to protecting workers whose skills are at risk of obsolescence because of large-scale technological transformation but also with respect to helping workers acquire new knowledge to keep pace with innovation, and thereby to increase worker bargaining power.

Efforts by labor unions to protect workers from technological displacement can be fraught, in some cases resulting in deep resistance to technological change. Numerous studies have captured this tension-filled relationship between technology development and labor advocacy, but this is not the only story in play. For the purposes of this chapter, it is more useful to consider concurrent actions by labor unions to get out in front of technological development in ways that recognize the uneven effects of innovation on the incumbent workforce.

One important historical case involved the 1959 "mechanization and modernization" deal struck between one of America's largest dockworker unions and a prominent shipping industry association to address the introduction of shipping containers at commercial ports on the West Coast. Containerization represented a major threat to tens of thousands of dockworkers (also known as longshoremen) who moved goods manually from the hulls of shipping vessels to neighboring freight yards. Incremental improvements to the established "breaking bulk" system, whereby longshoremen would manually unpack and repack shipping cargo, had been introduced over the decades, but still the "handling of cargo was almost as labor intensive after World War II as it was during the beginning of the Victorian age."[6]

Containerization would change all that in ways that, at the time, were perceived to be as radical and disruptive as driverless vehicles are today. With this technological shift, goods that arrived in a port would remain in a pre-packed metal box, to be moved by a series of cranes and related ground equipment from ship to truck or train—an intermodal method initially proposed by Malcolm McLean, a trucking entrepreneur from North Carolina who sought a more effective means to integrate shipping and long-haul trucking systems. Once adopted, containerization would eliminate the need for workers to manually load cargo.[7] Containerization would eventually become a catalyst to global trade,[8] but in 1959 America, the more immediate concern was reduced labor demand.

Under the leadership of Harry Bridges, the International Longshoremen's and Warehousemen's Union (ILWU) decided early on not to resist the introduction of container technology outright. But the ILWU only agreed to do so in exchange for a steady-paced phase-in of the technology that would stretch out over the course of a decade and give union leaders greater say in its rollout. Not surprisingly, tensions arose between labor and management during this protracted transition, especially when some shipping companies breached safety procedures and put workers at partially upgraded facilities at greater risk of injury. Still, by the end the decade, the technology was adopted, but with mechanisms in place to protect the economic security of thousands of older port workers and related provisions to support career mobility for younger ones.[9] Put simply, the modernization agreement parsed longshoremen by seniority, giving those already on track to retire by the late 1960s even better pensions, topped with generous phase-out pay. More than creating a social safety net, however, it also established a robust training fund and upskilling system to ensure the next generation of longshoremen had lucrative career options in logistics management and maintenance of port technology.

In-depth analyses of the ILWU agreement—and a related one signed by unions and shipping employers in 1963 in British Columbia, Canada—not only indicate a sizable bump in productivity at participating West Coast ports (7 percent for the United States, 7.4 percent in Canada) but, equally important, better incomes for unionized port workers.[10] As one economist put it, "The change … has benefited all parties—the longshoreman through enhanced incomes and benefits, the employers through lower costs and the public through the provision of more efficient longshore services at lower cost."[11]

In Las Vegas, a modern-day equivalent of a similar technology-focused labor agreement is now in place, thanks to the pioneering efforts of the city's combined culinary and bartender unions (Culinary Union, for short), which collectively represent over 57,000 hospitality workers. The Culinary Union—a local affiliate of the national umbrella organization UNITE HERE—has long supported workers in Las Vegas's casino industry, creating structures that advance workers in housekeeping, food service, entertainment, and event planning through a well-illuminated career pipeline with clear wage progression and extensive benefits. Their efforts enable most casino workers to enjoy a middle-class lifestyle supported by well-paying, rewarding jobs. And the union's commitment to workforce development, including its management of an industry-backed training fund, has produced substantial benefits for the employing casinos. Las Vegas not only boasts a highly productive hospitality sector, it also receives consistently high marks for quality customer service, thereby enabling it to outcompete other hospitality destinations for high-profile, big-ticket events.[12]

In the mid-2000s, members of the Culinary Union began raising concerns about the future impact of automation on casino jobs.[13] Though automation is still treated as a novelty, a number of casinos have rolled out high-tech services in hopes of luring tech-savvy, millennial-age customers. One example is Tipsy, a fully automated bar where customers enter their drink orders on a digital tablet, sending instructions to two robotic arms that mix drinks as a human bartender would and place the finished cocktails on a modern-day version of a mechanical sorting belt. At least one Vegas casino offers the option for automated room service, with motorized programmable devices navigating the halls and elevators to deliver food from the hotel kitchen to guest rooms, a mobile technology similar to that now used to deliver pizzas in select urban neighborhoods in the United States.

These high-tech applications—and others that, for now, are in a formative stage—motivated the Culinary Union to include an explicit technology provision in their latest contract.[14] Similar to the ILWU's contract seventy years before, this agreement includes a technology pacing component, in this case a requirement that Vegas-based casinos notify unions well in advance of technology implementation—a minimum of 180 days' (or six months') notice. The reasoning is that early notice will give unions time to investigate the potential impact of a technological change on the current workforce and to devise adaptive responses, including the option to bargain for additional time and better worker outcomes.[15] Here too, the unions leverage a well-funded training program to round out workforce skill, especially for workers whose jobs are locked in the cross-hairs of new technology, giving those most at risk of job loss greater latitude to move to a safer occupational perch.

The Vegas unions' approach also includes an important twist not included in the 1950s port arrangement—an additional step that represents a novel response to new technology development. The Culinary Union introduced an annual survey to elevate the visibility of front-line worker knowledge in new technology development and deployment. More than just reacting to a proposed technological change, its goal is to solicit worker input on problems that most need sophisticated technology solutions. The union-administered annual survey asks all members for feedback on the problems they encounter in their daily work and captures ideas for possible fixes.

The union's first survey revealed two promising technological innovations. The first was battery-operated carts that housekeeping staff could control electronically, reducing the physical toll from pushing heavy carts overloaded with vacuum cleaners, fresh linens, and other required supplies down long hotel corridors. The second was GPS-enabled panic buttons that could be attached to or embedded in the uniform to protect workers, especially women, from sexual or physical assault.

How might this survey translate into better working conditions? Labor economist Richard Freeman has recently suggested that for workers to capture more of the gains from technological change, they need to become direct owners of capital,[16] either by starting worker-owned enterprises to commercialize new technologies or by having a greater stake in the financing decisions that support technology development, including the investment choices of worker pension funds. In this context, the technology survey developed by the Culinary Union offers a means to facilitate ownership by identifying new technological applications that could be developed through worker-owned enterprises or even as generators of revenue for the union through technology licensing.

But creating a formal ownership stake for front-line workers is only one means to democratize technology choice and temper its labor market impact. The Las Vegas and port worker cases point to additional, complementary steps. Both illustrate the buffering role of high-quality vocational training—not just retraining displaced workers for jobs in other sectors, as is often pushed by technologists, but proactive, technology-responsive training that reinforces job mobility for incumbent workers in the same occupational or organizational setting. These cases also highlight the potential for institutional actors to negotiate the pace of technological adoption, using this to create breathing room to devise worker-friendly solutions. While not stalling technological process entirely, a negotiated strategy can be used to align worker and industry interests. It offers a pacing tactic to ensure workers are not overlooked in the frenzied rush (or race) to incorporate the latest technological breakthrough or fad. Businesses may also reap benefits from taking additional time to consider the effects of technology on business operations and occupational mobility.

But the Culinary Union case evidences a third target for institutional action, one designed to elevate the contribution of front-line worker knowledge to shaping formative technologies. As illustrated by the Culinary Union's technology survey, labor advocates do not need to cede technology expertise to tech companies that have neither a strong connection to their region nor concern for local working conditions. They can instead position front-line workers as domain experts empowered to influence which technology solutions should be prioritized in line with worker experience and needs. In this respect, front-line worker expertise augments technology development and deployment, helping bring to light serious productivity problems in need of improvement and also guiding innovators to focus their creative energy in support of job-enhancing solutions.

But even with successful examples like these to emulate, it would be a mistake to place responsibility for the future of work entirely in the hands of labor unions—and, by implication, to suggest that workforce intermediaries need only seek out partnerships with unions to influence the pace and intensity of technology development. It is important to note that the labor unions that successfully pushed technology provisions into collective bargaining agreements, both in Las Vegas and earlier at the West Coast shipping ports, were already well established labor representatives. Both unions had decades of experience forging industry connections and defending the skills contribution of their vast membership base. And both started from a strong bargaining position and leveraged it to gain influence over emerging technology choices and decisions.

These conditions are not always true of labor unions in the United States, particularly in regions that have had to defend against sustained political attacks on organized labor. And many regions have limited labor union involvement, with union density at less than 3 percent of the workforce in certain southern states, including North Carolina, where I live. This reality necessitates broadening the scope beyond unions to include other institutional partners to help expand this inclusive innovation space. With this in mind, I turn next to several examples that involve innovation-supporting universities and federal research laboratories, recognizing their role in pioneering next-generation technologies and their increased interest in influencing business development in ways that ensure workers share the benefits of technological progress.

## Technology Codesign

As an alumna of MIT, I receive a monthly copy of *Technology Review* magazine, cherishing its arrival and the insights it provides into emerging and cutting-edge technologies developed by other MIT alumni or the institute's faculty, students, or postdoctoral fellows. One issue from summer 2018 stood out from others I received that year, not because it revealed another awe-inspiring innovation or transformational technology but because it shed light on the need for greater institutional oversight and guidance in support of new technology development.

It included a brief but poignant essay by Erin Winick, the magazine's associate editor for the future of work. In it, she describes a memorable summer internship when she was a rising third-year college student based in Southern California. As an engineering intern at a midsize manufacturing firm, Erin was asked by the company owner to devise a novel 3D printing solution for a complex mold-making process. She soon realized that her solution, when implemented, would negatively affect one incumbent worker at the factory, rendering his two-decade career in mold-making outdated and obsolete. As she notes in her heartfelt essay, aptly titled "Confessions of an Accidental Job Destroyer," "He had spent over 20 years perfecting these tools and parts. If my project succeeded, I would be making him redundant."[17]

This simple yet courageous act of publicly affirming one's own role in job destruction has the potential to motivate a much wider discussion within universities about the ethical responsibility of student and faculty innovators. One could easily imagine an ethics section focused on new technology and the future of work inserted into an existing engineering or computer science seminar—or, better yet, a curriculum modification, resulting in all students within a subset of majors completing a course on technology and society. In fact, ethics training is now under consideration as a requirement for professional accreditation in engineering—though admittedly, at least for now, there is not an explicit focus on labor market outcomes. Still, this development suggests an opening for US-based universities to encode a moral standard when preparing students to enter technology-focused careers.

But beyond the implications for classroom ethics and curricular design, Erin's essay is even more telling for the clues it provides for targeted institutional action on the business side. She shares the troubling realization that her summer employer seemed less than forthcoming with existing workers about the job-displacing effects of her technology fix; by default, her coworkers assumed there was limited employer interest in engaging front-line workers in the innovation process. Gary, the worker with the most at stake, noted, "The 'official position' of the company was that there was no attempt to change anything about how things were being done."[18] In other words, the impact of this novel technological application on the current workforce was of little concern.

Faced with this dilemma, Erin informally reached out to Gary during the course of her internship to first gauge his knowledge of 3D printing, in the hope of establishing a role for him in technology implementation. Years later she contacted him again, and learned he had felt pressured to leave the company soon after her internship ended, following in the footsteps of other displaced manufacturing workers who have faced similarly jarring midcareer transitions (Gary now works in customer service).

But could Gary's fate have changed if institutional actors—rather than Erin, a student intern—were in the role of mediating technology uptake and deployment at this particular firm and other manufacturing establishments like it? What if these same institutional actors had helped highlight the valuable experience and expertise that Gary and other front-line workers at the company could bring to technology development and diffusion, not only informing areas in need of new technology solutions but also revealing constraints on wider acceptance or adoption that might not have been visible to owners or top-level executives? And what further gains in business performance and innovation could this greater commitment to worker inclusion and participation have generated?

Fortunately, there are several examples of business-facing institutions in the United States that have sought to play this type of mediating role, both in response to earlier transformative technologies and in light of emerging ones today. While Gary's job was outside their reach, their existence suggests the possibility of generating better alternatives for other potentially vulnerable manufacturing workers, and to do so in ways that also benefit the firms that employ them.

One institution active in this space and on the radar of many workforce advocates is the US Manufacturing Extension Partnership (MEP), a state-spanning network of extension organizations that receives state and federal funding to work with small and medium-sized manufacturing firms. State and local MEPs offer client businesses a wide array of manufacturing improvement solutions, some of which focus on new technology assessment and incorporation. As noted in chapter 3, thought leaders in the workforce world are encouraging workforce intermediaries to establish more robust partnerships with their local MEP centers. Illustrative cases already exist that help to motivate more action in this area, including the example of the Illinois Manufacturing Excellence Center (IMEC), mentioned in chapter 3, which has developed a pioneering approach to engaging manufacturing businesses to improve job quality for front-line production workers.[19] As IMEC works with firms to improve the work environment and use better talent management to advance firm performance, it has found ways to connect with a growing set of Chicago-based workforce intermediaries, including the Jane Addams Resource Center, Bethel New Life, and Opportunity Advancement Innovation. In 2020, another promising alliance between workforce intermediaries and manufacturing extension providers was forged, called the Industry and Inclusion 4.0 cohort—this one with an explicit racial equity goal. Leveraging Lumina Foundation funding, this initiative is designed to pair the programming and learning outcomes of several prominent workforce intermediaries featured in this book (the Wisconsin Regional Training Partnership, introduced in chapter 3, and the Chicago Manufacturing Renaissance Council, featured in chapter 4) with manufacturing support services offered through Cleveland's MAGNET MEP and Chicago's ManufacturingUSA Institute, MxD.

More partnering like this with local MEP centers creates an additional opening for workforce intermediaries to insert themselves into an even broader innovation network. Nationally, MEP is a critical partner in the ManufacturingUSA network, 14 federally funded technology institutes, including MxD in Chicago, that were established during the Obama administration to forge stronger connections between research universities, government agencies, and US-based manufacturing businesses. Each institute in the network focuses on a transformative technology, ranging from additive manufacturing and 3D printing (America Makes in Youngstown, Ohio) and biofabrication (BioFabUSA in Manchester, New Hampshire) to photonics (AIM Photonics in Rochester, New York) and advanced robotics (ARM in Pittsburgh, Pennsylvania). The main goal of these institutes is to streamline technology commercialization, bringing prospective manufacturing users of new technology into direct contact with innovators and forging cross-sectoral connections to increase the likelihood that innovations in advanced technology will align with the real challenges and needs facing American firms.[20]

In 2016, funding support was created to embed MEP technology experts within each of these institutes in an effort to transmit vital information about new technological developments to local MEP member organizations. With this added layer of institutional support, the hope was for small- and medium-sized manufacturers to adopt new technologies that would drive product and process innovation. While a path for workforce intermediaries to build on MEP connections and push into the ManufacturingUSA network is nowhere close to established, there are glimpses of what could be done to better leverage this opportunity.

Several of the ManufacturingUSA institutes have an explicit workforce development mission, creating room for staff with MEP connections to partner with local workforce intermediaries, including community colleges, to help incumbent manufacturing workers gain access to training in support of technology diffusion. As one example, MEP-affiliated staff within the PowerAmerica Institute in North Carolina are working with two state-funded community colleges to create new certificate programs in support of a high-performance technology called wide-bandgap semiconductors. This technology is proving critical for powering energy-efficient construction equipment and electric vehicles and is therefore an obvious skill development target for the advanced manufacturing workforce.

Another ManufacturingUSA institute, Advanced Robotics for Manufacturing, or ARM, in Pittsburgh, launched a collaborative project with MIT in 2017 to develop a novel Teach-Bot application to "lower barriers to entry" in industrial robotics for both incumbent and aspiring manufacturing workers. In this case, the robot is not just a new technology to be learned, it is also designed to be the trainer. As it interacts with production workers it supports technology understanding through demonstration, creating an interactive learning environment that is not dependent on workers having coding knowledge or previous robotics know-how.[21]

North Carolina's MEP is also tapping ARM Institute's expertise in advanced robotics. In February 2019, they cohosted an informational event at North Carolina State University to help MEP staff in North Carolina learn more about collaborative robot (cobot) use within smaller-sized manufacturing facilities. In contrast to more standard robotics applications, cobots offer smaller firms greater flexibility, including safety mechanisms that support ongoing human interaction. These features, along with their lower price tag, make cobots a potentially better fit for small and midsize manufacturers than larger, specialized robotic systems.

By supporting greater uptake of cobots in US manufacturing, North Carolina's MEP is helping lay the groundwork for robotics technologies that enhance rather than displace the existing manufacturing workforce. And this means there is also an opportunity for further institutional coordination, leveraging government-funded support for advanced manufacturing to promote job-protecting uses of automation. This outcome has reinforced the intermediaries' role in helping smaller manufacturers recognize the value of including front-line workers in the codesign of technology-based solutions.

Another exemplary early effort is a state-funded technology center in Buffalo, New York, that has worked with at least one manufacturing company to design a cobot in partnership with manufacturing workers. This partnership grew in response to worker frustration with small-parts assembly at a local laptop manufacturing company. Supported by the employer, a team of production workers paired up with industrial engineers and technologists at the Manufacturing Works technology center to create a cobot production assistant. As a leader at Manufacturing Works explained, no manufacturing jobs were shed as a result of this technology-development process; rather, the production team expanded from five to six members, with the cobot the added sixth team member. And while the idea of involving front-line production workers in technology design initially came from a set of enlightened business owners, the state-funded technology center at the heart of this effort is now positioned to advocate for participatory design, extending this model of worker engagement as it supports other small and medium-sized manufacturing firms in the region.

The recently formed Industry and Inclusion 4.0 cohort shows it is possible for contemporary workforce intermediaries to formally collaborate with innovation-focused institutions—but what that means at the worker-technology interface is yet to be determined. One initiative from the past offers an inspiring model for what this institutional collaboration could look like going forward. In the late 1980s a labor union in Massachusetts helped a midsize manufacturing firm connect with a new state-funded initiative called the Center for Applied Technology (CAT). With union support, CAT staff were able to forge a joint worker-management team to improve productivity and quality control, including extending training supports to encourage production worker involvement. The union's role was to push for "equality of knowledge," ensuring workers were recognized as true participants in technology development and implementation.[22]

Launched in 1987, CAT was pioneering and forward-thinking, with an explicit worker-supporting objective: to "enhance worker skill; allow users to interact more creatively with machines/software; increase/enhance health and safety; encourage cooperative forms of work organization."[23] Labor union involvement not only reinforced CAT's core mission to bring workers into the technology fold, it also created an institutional structure for bringing business owners and managers to the table. This example suggests there is ample room for modern-day workforce institutions—union-affiliated or not—to formally partner with today's advanced technology centers, including ones that are university-based, to push for wider adoption of participatory design principles and elevate the contribution of experienced production workers in the process. Ultimately, this mediating role would ensure workers are not just distantly informing technology choices but are valued partners in innovation, offering shop floor insights and smarts to guide technological progress.

## Resilient Cities

Despite the institutional focus of the book up to this point, truly placing front-line workers at the center of technology-based decision-making means reaching well beyond the boundaries of technology-focused institutions, whether federally funded institutes or prominent research universities. It also means acquiring real influence within a broader policy framework to shape how technology is used and deployed in support of critical social, economic, and environmental objectives. This speaks to a third target for coordinated institutional action and advocacy: leveraging support for regional infrastructure and environmentally friendly urban innovations to promote more inclusive standards for the development of resilient cities.[24]

Numerous cities in the United States are putting their weight behind climate resilience and energy efficiency, committing political leadership and vast quantities of public funding to drive innovative solutions that will shape future urban and regional development. As part of this "clean" and "resilient city" movement, progressive coalitions are forming with the goal of supporting greater economic inclusion in this transition. In some cases, this includes advocacy to ensure public funds are not used to "incentivize" job displacement via adoption of high-tech innovations but rather mandate inclusion through formal contracts secured through a reinforcing web of workforce agreements and local sourcing requirements.

An inspiring illustration is a multicity initiative recently launched by the social justice coalition Jobs to Move America. This coalition has secured commitments from planning and transit agencies in roughly ten cities, including Los Angeles, Chicago, and Seattle, to ensure large-scale public transportation projects generate significant employment gains and career-enhancing opportunities for low-income residents.[25] Part of the Jobs to Move America toolkit is the US Employment Plan, a policy and evaluation framework that worker advocates can draw on to promote job access and skill development in their respective cities.

Pre-approved by the US Department of Labor, the US Employment Plan offers a replicable model for managing procurement processes in urban transportation. In Los Angeles, the adoption of the US Employment Plan as the default template for practice means extending worker benefits across the entire transit supply chain; with this agreement in place, city planners are now able to award contracts to clean-transit manufacturers on the basis of creating good jobs locally. But the Jobs to Move America coalition also recognizes that for urban commitments to electric transit systems and related applications of clean technology to extend economic opportunity, employer investments in workforce skill development are also critical, and so they add the important proviso that public contracting also favor manufacturers that offer their workforce on-the-job training.[26]

What makes the US Employment Plan an especially promising vehicle for scaling up workforce intermediation efforts is the additional involvement by local community and labor coalitions in shaping the conditions for plan implementation. In Chicago, for example, a 2016 contract for the "el" involved a South Side community-labor coalition that worked to ensure the four hundred manufacturing and warehouse jobs created were inclusive of low-income residents from the surrounding neighborhood.[27] Building on the US Employment Plan, the coalition pushed the city to adopt a "community benefits"[28] addendum that would guarantee jobs for South Side residents, with public-private funding commitments to support skill development through apprenticeship and work-based learning. As this development suggests, Jobs to Move America is helping create an inclusive framework to draw workforce advocates into the urban policymaking arena. And this creates the potential for workforce intermediaries to not just shape job access within energy-efficient transportation but also affect related decisions around how other energy-saving technologies are used by American cities to align environmental and equity goals.

### A Moral Commitment to Inclusive Innovation

Traditional and social media are abuzz with concerns that disruptive technologies are on a direct collision course with America's blue-collar workforce, with catastrophic implications for economic mobility. Whether the focus is autonomous vehicles, robotics, or other applications in artificial intelligence, there is growing concern over the potential for widespread job displacement, with some alarming estimates putting close to 50 percent of the US workforce in peril.[29] Reports from the initial months of the COVID-19 pandemic have reinforced this imagined future, some claiming technologies will be adopted even faster to lower the contagion risk associated with human worker involvement. A number of interesting solutions have been circulating of late, ranging from supply-side retraining efforts to stronger social safety nets. But while these proposals might look quite different, they are often predicated on the troubling assumption that technological progress is an unstoppable high-speed express train, with restricted access and little room to maneuver to slow things down.[30]

This chapter has offered some promising examples that, in combination, speak to a very different technological future: one in which technological advances do not mercilessly gut the current workforce, with little care for those already struggling to make ends meet, but instead recognize blue-collar front-line workers as central actors in technological decision-making and implementation. In this alternative future, workers are sought out for their participation and involvement and recognized for their critical experience and expertise, which will help sustain industry innovation and upgrading. Rather than pushing aside or further marginalizing the blue-collar workforce, these innovative solutions are worker-inclusive and seek to extend similar opportunities to job seekers who might otherwise be in a vulnerable economic position. And this involvement of front-line workers is not just a critical means for tempering the displacing effects of technology at work; it reflects a democratized approach to decision-making that can also provide a vehicle for addressing other pressing societal needs or concerns, climate change among them.

More than a utopian vision, the examples in this chapter show that real progress is being made through grassroots organizing led by forward-thinking labor advocates and through pioneering initiatives by research institutions and leading-edge technology centers. Beyond simply elevating the visibility of these localized experiments, I share these stories to inspire further institutional and political action on which to build a stronger moral and social commitment to inclusive innovation. For business owners, these cases illuminate broader possibilities beyond the false choice of job shedding or technological stagnation. For scholars, they point to the value of digging deeper into grounded cases where work and technology actually interact[31]—countering claims by technology firms and their financial backers of a workless future by unpacking the micropolitics of technology adoption as lived through the worker experience.[32] For labor advocates, they are a call to increase public awareness of the dramatically different technology models that exist even within seemingly narrow technological areas, thus expanding the scope for institutional action well beyond an overhaul of national regulations or the corporate taxation code.

The cases presented in this chapter also elevate the creative and evolving strategies that workforce institutions can use to gain greater influence over technological choices within communities and workplaces, helping determine which technologies get adopted, at which point in time, and with which economic and social interests in mind. If our technological future is limitless, so too are the institutional responses that will give it direction and meaning. The workforce intermediaries featured in this book are refining front-line strategies to engage firms in a negotiated process around skill. And by shaping the skills that will drive innovation in the future, they are not just preparing the twenty-first-century workforce, they are pushing higher standards for an even better workplace.

# Notes

## Chapter 1

1. Anthony P. Carnevale, Jeff Strohl, and Artem Gulish, *College Is Just the Beginning: Employers' Role in the $1.1 Trillion Postsecondary Education and Training System* (Washington, DC: Georgetown University Center on Education and the Workforce, 2015); Kelly S. Mikelson and Demetra Nightingale, "Estimating Public and Private Expenditures on Occupational Training in the United States" (Washington, DC: Urban Institute, 2004).

2. Lisa M. Lynch and Sandra E. Black, "Beyond the Incidence of Employer-Provided Training," *ILR Review* 52, no. 1 (1998): 64–81; Robert I. Lerman, Signe-Mary McKernan, and Stephanie Riegg, "The Scope of Private Sector Training: Who, What, Where, and How Much?," in *Job Training Policy in the United States*, ed. Christopher O'Leary, Robert A. Straits, and Stephen A. Wandner (Kalamazoo, MI: Upjohn Institute, 2004), 211–244; Harley J. Frazis, Diane E. Herz, and Michael W. Horrigan, "Employer-Provided Training: Results from a New Survey," *Monthly Labor Review* 118 (1995): 3.

3. Andrew Weaver and Paul Osterman, "Skill Demands and Mismatch in US Manufacturing," *ILR Review* 70, no. 2 (2017): 275–307.

4. Suzanne Berger, *Making in America: From Innovation to Market* (Cambridge, MA: MIT Press, 2013); Eileen Appelbaum and Rosemary Batt, *Private Equity at Work: When Wall Street Manages Main Street* (New York: Russell Sage Foundation, 2014).

5. David Weil, *The Fissured Workplace* (Cambridge, MA: Harvard University Press, 2014); Susan Helper "Supply Chains and Equitable Growth" (Washington D.C.: Washington Center for Equitable Growth, 2016).

6. Lisa M. Lynch, "Development Intermediaries and the Training of Low-Wage Workers," in *Emerging Labor Market Institutions for the Twenty-First Century*, ed. Richard B. Freeman, Joni Hersch, and Lawrence Mishel (Chicago: University of Chicago Press, 2004), 293–314.

7. Adam Davidson, "Making It in America," *Atlantic*, February 2012.

8. Danielle Allen, "What Is Education For?," *Boston Review*, May 2016; Walter W. McMahon, *Higher Learning, Greater Good: The Private and Social Benefits of Higher Education* (Baltimore, MD: Johns Hopkins University Press, 2009); David E. Bloom, Matthew Hartley, and Henry Rosovsky, "Beyond Private Gain: The Public Benefits of Higher Education," in *International Handbook of Higher Education* (New York: Springer, 2007), 293–308.

9. David Cooper, Lawrence Mishel, and Ben Zipperer, "Bold Increases in the Minimum Wage Should Be Evaluated for the Benefits of Raising Low-Wage Workers' Total Earnings: Critics Who Cite Claims of Job Loss Are Using a Distorted Frame" (Washington, DC: Economic Policy Institute, 2018).

10. David Card and Alan B. Krueger, "Time-Series Minimum-Wage Studies: A Meta-Analysis," *American Economic Review* 85, no. 2 (1995): 238–243; Arindrajit Dube, T. William Lester, and Michael Reich, "Minimum Wage Effects across State Borders: Estimates Using Contiguous Counties," *Review of Economics and Statistics* 92, no. 4 (2010): 945–964.

11. T. William Lester, "Restructuring Restaurant Work: Employer Responses to Local Labor Standards in the Full-Service Restaurant Industry," *Urban Affairs Review* 56, no. 2 (2020): 605–639.

12. Ben Casselman, "Robots or Job Training: Manufacturers Grapple with How to Improve Their Economic Fortunes," *New York Times*, June 25, 2018.

13. Doruk Cengiz, Arindrajit Dube, Attila Lindner, and Ben Zipperer, *The Effect of Minimum Wages on Low-Wage Jobs: Evidence from the United States Using a Bunching Estimator* (London: London School of Economics and Political Science, Centre for Economic Performance, 2018).

14. Arne L. Kalleberg, *Good Jobs, Bad Jobs: The Rise of Polarized and Precarious Employment Systems in the United States, 1970s–2000s* (New York: Russell Sage Foundation, 2011); Paul Osterman and Beth Shulman, *Good Jobs America* (New York: Russell Sage Foundation, 2011); Zeynep Ton, *The Good Jobs Strategy: How the Smartest Companies Invest in Employees to Lower Costs and Boost Profits* (New York: Houghton Mifflin Harcourt, 2014); Rick Wartzman, *The End of Loyalty: The Rise and Fall of Good Jobs in America* (New York: PublicAffairs, 2017).

15. The concept of ambiguity features centrally in theories of innovation and has informed my thinking about its connection to skill. See Richard K. Lester and Michael J. Piore, *Innovation: The Missing Dimension* (Cambridge: Harvard University Press, 2009); David Stark, *The Sense of Dissonance: Accounts of Worth in Economic Life* (Princeton, NJ: Princeton University Press, 2011).

16. Paul Osterman, "Institutional Labor Economics, the New Personnel Economics, and Internal Labor Markets: A Reconsideration," *ILR Review* 64, no. 4 (July 2011): 637–653.

17. Robert P. Giloth, ed., *Workforce Intermediaries: For the 21st Century* (Philadelphia: Temple University Press, 2010).

18. Lawrence Mishel, "Yes, Manufacturing Still Provides a Pay Advantage, but Staffing Firm Outsourcing Is Eroding It" (Washington, DC: Economic Policy Institute, March 12, 2018).

19. Wartzman, *The End of Loyalty*.

20. Susan N. Houseman, "Understanding the Decline of U.S. Manufacturing Employment" (Kalamazoo, MI: W. E. Upjohn Institute, 2018); Daron Acemoglu, David Autor, David Dorn, et al., "Return of the Solow Paradox? IT, Productivity, and Employment in US Manufacturing," *American Economic Review* 104, no. 5 (2014): 394–399; David Autor, David Dorn, and Gordon Hanson, "When Work Disappears: Manufacturing Decline and the Falling Marriage-Market Value of Young Men," *American Economic Review: Insights* 1, no. 2 (2018): 161–178; Teresa C. Fort, Justin R. Pierce, and Peter K. Schott, "New Perspectives on the Decline of US Manufacturing Employment," *Journal of Economic Perspectives* 32, no. 2 (2018): 47–72.

21. Louis Uchitelle, *Making It: Why Manufacturing Still Matters* (New York: New Press, 2017); Berger, *Making in America*.

22. Houseman, "Understanding the Decline of U.S. Manufacturing Employment."

23. Robert D. Atkinson, "Which Nations Really Lead in Industrial Robot Adoption?" (Washington, DC: Information Technology and Innovation Foundation, November 2018); Robert D. Atkinson and Adams Nager, "Can US Manufacturing Be Made Great Again?," *Industry Week*, February 22, 2017.

24. Giloth, *Workforce Intermediaries;* Maureen Conway and Robert P. Giloth, "Introduction," in *Connecting People to Work: Workforce Intermediaries and Sector Strategies,* ed. Maureen Conway and Robert P. Giloth (New York: American Assembly and Columbia University, 2014), 1–19; Brenda Lautsch and Paul Osterman, "Changing the Constraints: A Successful Employment and Training Strategy," *Jobs and Economic Development: Strategies and Practice,* ed. Robert P. Giloth (Newbury Park, CA: Sage, 1998), 214–233; Greg Schrock, "Reworking Workforce Development: Chicago's Sectoral Workforce Centers," *Economic Development Quarterly* 27, no. 3 (2013): 163–178; Maureen Conway, *The Garment Industry Development Corporation: A Case Study of a Sectoral Employment Development Approach*, Sectoral Employment Development Learning Project Case Studies Series (New York: Aspen Institute, 1999); Maureen Conway, Linda Dworak-Muñoz, and Amy Blair, "Sectoral Workforce Development: Research Review and Future Directions" (Washington, DC: Aspen Institute, 2004).

25. Conway and Giloth, "Introduction."

26. Maureen Conway and Steven Dawson, "Restore the Promise of Work: Reducing Inequality by Raising the Floor and Building Ladders" (Washington, DC: Aspen Institute, April 13, 2016).

27. Steven Greenhouse, *Beaten Down, Worked Up: The Past, Present, and Future of American Labor* (New York: Knopf Doubleday Publishing Group, 2019).

28. Natasha Iskander and Nichola Lowe, "Immigration and the Politics of Skill," in *The New Oxford Handbook of Economic Geography*, ed. Gordon L. Clark, Maryann P. Feldman, Meric S. Gertler, and Dariusz Wojcik (Oxford: Oxford University Press, 2018), 519–536.

29. Shoshana Zuboff, *In the Age of the Smart Machine: The Future of Work and Power* (New York: Basic Books, 1988), 7.

30. Michael Burawoy, "From Polanyi to Pollyanna: The False Optimism of Global Labor Studies," *Global Labour Journal* 1, no. 2 (May 31, 2010); Paul S. Adler, "The Future of Critical Management Studies: A Paleo-Marxist Critique of Labour Process Theory," *Organization Studies* 28, no. 9 (2007): 1313–1345; Natasha Iskander and Nichola Lowe, "Building Job Quality from the Inside-Out: Mexican Immigrants, Skills, and Jobs in the Construction Industry," *Industrial and Labor Relations Review* 66, no. 4 (2013): 785–807.

31. Martin Kenney and John Zysman, "The Rise of the Platform Economy," *Issues in Science and Technology* 32, no. 3 (2016): 61; Rian Whitton, "Automation Anxiety in an Age of Stagnation," *American Affairs* 3, no. 2 (Summer 2019): 25–42.

## Chapter 2

1. OECD, "Inequality Update," November 2016, https://www.oecd.org/social/OECD 2016-Income-Inequality-Update.pdf.

2. Elise Gould, "Wage Inequality Continued Its 35-Year Rise in 2015," Briefing Paper 421 (Washington, DC: Economic Policy Institute, 2016); Jeff Larrimore et al., "Report on the Economic Well-Being of U.S. Households in 2017" (Washington, DC.: Board of Governors for the Federal Reserve System, May 2018).

3. Heather Boushey, *Unbound: How Inequality Constricts Our Economy and What We Can Do about It* (Cambridge, MA: Harvard University Press, 2019).

4. Steve J. Davis and John Haltiwanger, "Wage Dispersion between and within US Manufacturing Plants, 1963–1986," NBER Working Paper 3722 (Cambridge, MA: National Bureau of Economic Research, 1991).

5. Zvi Griliches, "Capital-Skill Complementarity," *Review of Economics and Statistics*, 1969, 465–468.

6. Villy Bergstrom and Epaminondas E. Panas, "How Robust Is the Capital-Skill Complementarity Hypothesis?," *Review of Economics and Statistics* 74, no. 3 (1992): 540–546; Chinhui Juhn, Kevin M. Murphy, and Brooks Pierce, "Wage Inequality and the Rise in Returns to Skill," *Journal of Political Economy* 101, no. 3 (1993): 410–442.

7. Alan B. Krueger, "How Computers Have Changed the Wage Structure: Evidence from Microdata, 1984–1989," *Quarterly Journal of Economics* 108, no. 1 (1993): 33–60.

8. Frank Levy and Richard J. Murnane, "With What Skills Are Computers a Complement?," *American Economic Review* 86, no. 2 (1996): 258–262; David H. Autor, Frank Levy, and Richard J. Murnane, "The Skill Content of Recent Technological Change: An Empirical Exploration," *Quarterly Journal of Economics* 118, no. 4 (2003): 1279–1333.

9. Eli Berman, John Bound, and Stephen Machin, "Implications of Skill-Biased Technological Change: International Evidence," *Quarterly Journal of Economics* 113, no. 4 (1998): 1245–1279; Eli Berman, John Bound, and Zvi Griliches, "Changes in the Demand for Skilled Labor within US Manufacturing: Evidence from the Annual Survey of Manufactures," *Quarterly Journal of Economics* 109, no. 2 (1994): 367–397.

10. James Bessen, *Learning by Doing: The Real Connection between Innovation, Wages, and Wealth* (New Haven, CT: Yale University Press, 2015); Daron Acemoglu and David Autor, "Skills, Tasks and Technologies: Implications for Employment and Earnings," in *Handbook of Labor Economics*, vol. 4 (New York: Elsevier, 2011), 1043–1171; S. W. Elliot, "Projecting the Impact of Information Technology on Work and Skills in the 2030," in *The Oxford Handbook of Skills and Training*, ed. Chris Warhurst, Ken Mayhew, David Finegold, and John Buchanan (Oxford: Oxford University Press, 2017); David Autor, "Work of the Past, Work of the Future," NBER Working Paper 25588 (Cambridge, MA: National Bureau of Economic Research, 2019); Carl Benedik Frey, *The Technology Trap Capital, Labor, and Power in the Age of Automation* (Princeton, NJ: Princeton University Press, 2019).

11. Jinzhu Chen, Prakash Kannan, Prakash Loungani, and Bharat Trehan, "Cyclical or Structural? Evidence on the Sources of US Unemployment," in *Globalization: Strategies and Effects,* ed. Bent Jesper Christensen and Carsten Kowalczyk (New York: Springer, 2017), 245–264; Paul L. Daniels, Timothy O. Kestner, and Salvatore Lupica, "Structural Unemployment: A New Measurement and Continuing Discussion of an Elusive Economic Indicator" Virginia Employment Commission, Richmond, 2017; Thomas Janoski, David Luke, and Christopher Oliver, *The Causes of Structural Unemployment: Four Factors That Keep People from the Jobs They Deserve* (New York: John Wiley & Sons, 2014); Lawrence M. Kahn, *Skill Shortages, Mismatches, and Structural Unemployment: A Symposium* (Los Angeles: Sage, 2015); Pascual Restrepo, "Skill Mismatch and Structural Unemployment," Massachusetts Institute of Technology Job Market Paper, 2015, 1–94.

12. Acemoglu and Autor, "Skills, Tasks and Technologies"; David Autor, "The Polarization of Job Opportunities in the US Labor Market: Implications for Employment and Earnings," (Washington, DC: Center for American Progress—The Hamilton Project, 2010), 6; Harry J. Holzer and Robert I. Lerman, "America's Forgotten Middle-Skill Jobs" (Washington, DC: Urban Institute, 2007); Didem Tüzemen and Jonathan Willis, "The Vanishing Middle: Job Polarization and Workers' Response to the Decline in Middle-Skill Jobs," *Economic Review—Federal Reserve Bank of Kansas City*, 2013, 5.

13. David H. Autor, Lawrence F. Katz, and Melissa S. Kearney, "Trends in US Wage Inequality: Revising the Revisionists," *Review of Economics and Statistics* 90, no. 2 (2008): 300–323; Pew Research Center, "The American Middle Class Is Losing

Ground: No Longer the Majority and Falling behind Financially" (Washington, DC: Pew Research Center, December 2015).

14. Claudia Dale Goldin and Lawrence F. Katz, *The Race between Education and Technology* (Cambridge, MA: Harvard University Press, 2009).

15. Richard A. DeMillo and Andrew J. Young, *Revolution in Higher Education: How a Small Band of Innovators Will Make College Accessible and Affordable* (Cambridge, MA: MIT Press, 2015); Geoff Sharrock, "Making Sense of the MOOCs Debate," *Journal of Higher Education Policy and Management* 37, no. 5 (2015): 597–609; Michael Mitchell, Michael Leachman, and Kathleen Masterson, "A Lost Decade in Higher Education Funding State Cuts Have Driven up Tuition and Reduced Quality" (Washington, DC: Center on Budget and Policy Priorities, 2017).

16. Katherine S. Newman and Hella Winston, *Reskilling America: Learning to Labor in the Twenty-First Century* (New York: Metropolitan Books, 2016); Darryn Snell, "Vocational Education and the Revitalisation of Manufacturing in the United States," *Journal of Vocational Education & Training* 71, no. 2 (2019): 239–259; Anthony P. Carnevale, Tanya I. Garcia. Neil Ridley, and Michael C. Quinn, "The Overlooked Value of Certificates and Associate's Degrees" (Washington, DC: Georgetown University Center on Education and the Workforce, 2020); Henry Renski, "Estimating the Returns to Professional Certifications and Licenses in the US Manufacturing Sector," *Economic Development Quarterly* 32, no. 4 (2018): 341–356.

17. Paul Osterman, *Securing Prosperity: The American Labor Market: How It Has Changed and What to Do about It* (Princeton, NJ: Princeton University Press, 2000); David R. Howell, "Increasing Earnings Inequality and Unemployment in Developed Countries: Markets, Institutions, and the 'Unified Theory,'" *Politics & Society* 30, no. 2 (2002): 193–243; Frank Levy and Peter Temin, "Inequality and Institutions in Twentieth-Century America," *Economic Evolution and Revolution in Historical Time*, ed. Paul Rhode, Joshua Rosenbloom, and David Weiman (Stanford: Stanford University Press 2011).

18. David Howell, "Skills and the Wage Collapse: Better Education and Training Are Only Half the Story," *American Prospect* 11, no. 15 (2000): 74–77; David R. Howell, "Collapsing Wages and Rising Inequality: Has Computerization Shifted the Demand for Skills?," *Challenge* 38, no. 1 (1995): 27–35; David Card and John E. DiNardo, "Skill-Biased Technological Change and Rising Wage Inequality: Some Problems and Puzzles," *Journal of Labor Economics* 20, no. 4 (2002): 733–783.

19. Nancy Folbre, "Just Deserts? Earnings Inequality and Bargaining Power in the US Economy" (Washington, DC: Washington Center for Equitable Growth, 2016); Richard Freeman, "A Tale of Two Clones," Next, pt. 18, Third Way, September 27, 2016, https://www.thirdway.org/report/a-tale-of-two-clones.

20. Steven Greenhouse, *Beaten Down, Worked Up: The Past, Present, and Future of American Labor* (New York: Knopf Doubleday Publishing Group, 2019).

21. Osterman, *Securing Prosperity*; Paul Osterman and Beth Shulman, *Good Jobs America* (New York: Russell Sage Foundation, 2011); Neil Fligstein, "Social Skill and Institutional Theory," *American Behavioral Scientist* 40, no. 4 (February 1997): 397–405; Levy and Temin, "Inequality and Institutions in Twentieth-Century America"; Paul Osterman, Thomas A. Kochan, Richard M. Locke, and Michael J. Piore, *Working in America: A Blueprint for the New Labor Market* (Cambridge, MA: MIT Press, 2002).

22. Peter B. Doeringer and Michael J. Piore, *International Labor Markets and Manpower Analysis* (Lexington, MA: Heath Lexington Books, 1971).

23. Osterman, *Securing Prosperity*.

24. Rosabeth Moss Kanter, "The Middle Manager as Innovator," *Harvard Business Review* 60, no. 4 (1982): 95–105; William Lazonick, "Corporate Restructuring," in *The Oxford Handbook of Work and Organization*, ed. Stephen Ackroyd, Rosemary Batt, Paul Thompson, and Pamela S. Tolbert (Oxford: Oxford University Press, 2004), 576–601.

25. Rick Wartzman, *The End of Loyalty: The Rise and Fall of Good Jobs in America* (New York: PublicAffairs, 2017).

26. Daniel Markovits, "How McKinsey Destroyed the Middle Class: Technocratic Management, No Matter How Brilliant, Cannot Unwind Structural Inequalities," *Atlantic*, February 3, 2020.

27. Neil Fligstein and Taekjin Shin, "Shareholder Value and the Transformation of the US Economy, 1984–2000 1," *Sociological Forum* 22 (2007): 399–424; Rosemary Batt, Alexander J. S. Colvin, and Jeffrey Keefe, "Employee Voice, Human Resource Practices, and Quit Rates: Evidence from the Telecommunications Industry," *ILR Review* 55, no. 4 (2002): 573–594; Jacob S. Hacker and Paul Pierson, "Winner-Take-All Politics: Public Policy, Political Organization, and the Precipitous Rise of Top Incomes in the United States," *Politics & Society* 38, no. 2 (2010): 152–204; Francis Green, *Demanding Work: The Paradox of Job Quality in the Affluent Economy* (Princeton, NJ: Princeton University Press, 2006); Stephen R. Barley and Gideon Kunda, "Bringing Work Back In," *Organization Science* 12, no. 1 (2001): 76–95; Loïc Wacquant and John Howe, *Urban Outcasts: A Comparative Sociology of Advanced Marginality* (Cambridge: Polity Press, 2008); Arne L. Kalleberg, "Precarious Work, Insecure Workers: Employment Relations in Transition," *American Sociological Review* 74, no. 1 (2009): 1–22; Kalleberg, *Good Jobs, Bad Jobs*.

28. Osterman, *Securing Prosperity*.

29. Thomas A. Kochan and Saul A. Rubinstein, "Toward a Stakeholder Theory of the Firm: The Saturn Partnership," *Organization Science* 11, no. 4 (2000): 367–386; Thomas A. Kochan, Russell D. Lansbury, and John Paul MacDuffie, *After Lean Production: Evolving Employment Practices in the World Auto Industry* (Ithaca, NY: Cornell University Press, 1997), 33; Richard M. Locke, Thomas A. Kochan, and Michael J. Piore, *Employment Relations in a Changing World Economy* (Cambridge, MA: MIT Press, 1995).

30. John Paul MacDuffie and Thomas A. Kochan, "Do US Firms Invest Less in Human Resources? Training in the World Auto Industry," *Industrial Relations: A Journal of Economy and Society* 34, no. 2 (1995): 147–168.

31. Rosemary Batt and Eileen Appelbaum, *The New American Workplace: Transforming Work Systems in the United States* (Ithaca, NY: Cornell ILR Press, 1994); John Paul MacDuffie and Susan Helper, "Creating Lean Suppliers: Diffusing Lean Production through the Supply Chain," *California Management Review* 39, no. 4 (1997): 118–151; Susan Helper and Mari Sako, "Management Innovation in Supply Chain: Appreciating Chandler in the Twenty-First Century," *Industrial and Corporate Change* 19, no. 2 (2010): 399–429; Ruth Milkman, *Farewell to the Factory: Auto Workers in the Late Twentieth Century* (Berkeley and Los Angeles: University of California Press, 1997).

32. Ruth Milkman and Stephanie Luce, "Labor Unions and the Great Recession," *RSF: The Russell Sage Foundation Journal of the Social Sciences* 3, no. 3 (2017): 145–165; Arne L. Kalleberg and Till M. von Wachter, "The U.S. Labor Market During and After the Great Recession: Continuities and Transformations," *RSF: The Russell Sage Foundation Journal of the Social Sciences* 3, no. 3 (2017): 1.

33. Françoise Carré and Chris Tilly, *Where Bad Jobs Are Better: Retail Jobs across Countries and Companies* (New York: Russell Sage Foundation, 2017).

34. Ton, *The Good Jobs Strategy*.

35. Janice Fine and Jennifer Gordon, "Strengthening Labor Standards Enforcement through Partnerships with Workers' Organizations," *Politics & Society* 38, no. 4 (December 2010): 552–585; Nina Martin, "'There Is Abuse Everywhere': Migrant Nonprofit Organizations and the Problem of Precarious Work," *Urban Affairs Review* 48, no. 3 (2012): 389–416; Nina Martin, Sandra Morales, and Nik Theodore, "Migrant Worker Centers: Contending with Downgrading in the Low-Wage Labor Market," *GeoJournal* 68, nos. 2–3 (2007): 155–165; Annette Bernhardt, "The Role of Labor Market Regulation in Rebuilding Economic Opportunity in the United States," *Work and Occupations* 39, no. 4 (2012): 354–375; Annette D. Bernhardt, Heather Boushey, Laura Dresser, and Chris Tilly, eds., *The Gloves-off Economy: Workplace Standards at the Bottom of America's Labor Market* (Ithaca, NY: Cornell University Press, 2008); Weil, *The Fissured Workplace*; Jennifer Gordon, "Regulating the Human Supply Chain," *Iowa Law Review* 102 (2016): 445.

36. Marc Doussard and Ahmad Gamal, "The Rise of Wage Theft Laws: Can Community–Labor Coalitions Win Victories in State Houses?," *Urban Affairs Review* 52, no. 5 (2016): 780–807; Jamie Peck and Nik Theodore, "Contingent Chicago: Restructuring the Spaces of Temporary Labor," *International Journal of Urban and Regional Research* 25, no. 3 (2001): 471–496; Christian Zlolniski, *Janitors, Street Vendors, and Activists: The Lives of Mexican Immigrants in Silicon Valley* (Berkeley and Los Angeles: University of California Press, 2006).

37. Kalleberg, *Good Jobs, Bad Jobs*; Andy Stern, *Raising the Floor: How a Universal Basic Income Can Renew Our Economy and Rebuild the American Dream* (New York: PublicAffairs, 2016); Thomas A. Kochan and Lee Dyer, *Shaping the Future of Work: A Handbook for Action and a New Social Contract* (Cambridge, MA: MITx Press, 2017).

38. Annette Bernhardt and Paul Osterman, "Organizing for Good Jobs: Recent Developments and New Challenges," *Work and Occupations* 44, no. 1 (2017): 89–112; Stephanie Luce, Jennifer Luff, Joseph A. McCartin, and Ruth Milkman, eds., *What Works for Workers? Public Policies and Innovative Strategies for Low-Wage Workers* (New York: Russell Sage Foundation, 2014).

39. Weil, *The Fissured Workplace*; Louis Hyman, *Temp: How American Work, American Business, and the American Dream Became Temporary* (New York: Penguin, 2018); Jamie A. Peck and Nikolas Theodore, "Temped out? Industry Rhetoric, Labor Regulation and Economic Restructuring in the Temporary Staffing Business," *Economic and Industrial Democracy* 23, no. 2 (2002): 143–175; Christian Zlolniski, "Labor Control and Resistance of Mexican Immigrant Janitors in Silicon Valley," *Human Organization* 62, no. 1 (2003): 39.

40. Lawrence F. Katz and Alan B. Krueger, "The Rise and Nature of Alternative Work Arrangements in the United States, 1995–2015," *ILR Review* 72, no. 2 (2019): 382–416.

41. Weil, *The Fissured Workplace*; Steve Fraser, *The Age of Acquiescence: The Life and Death of American Resistance to Organized Wealth and Power* (Hachette UK, 2015); Thomas Geoghegan, *Only One Thing Can Save Us: Why America Needs a New Kind of Labor Movement* (New York: New Press, 2014); Hyman, *Temp*.

42. Appelbaum and Batt, *Private Equity at Work*.

43. Appelbaum and Batt, *Private Equity at Work* ; Weil, *The Fissured Workplace*.

44. Dube, Lester, and Reich, "Minimum Wage Effects across State Borders."

45. Thomas A. Kochan, *The Mutual Gains Enterprise: Forging a Winning Partnership among Labor, Management, and Government* (Boston: Harvard Business Press, 1994).

46. Doeringer and Piore, *International Labor Markets and Manpower Analysis*; Grace Palladino, *Skilled Hands, Strong Spirits: A Century of Building Trades History* (Ithaca, NY: Cornell University Press, 2005); Ruth Milkman and Kim Voss, *Rebuilding Labor: Organizing and Organizers in the New Union Movement* (Ithaca, NY: Cornell University Press, 2004).

47. Paul Attewell, "What Is Skill?," *Work and Occupations* 17, no. 4 (November 1990): 422–48; Irena Grugulis, Chris Warhurst, and Ewart Keep, "What's Happening to 'Skill,'" *The Skills That Matter*, 2004, 1–18; Michael Handel, "Trends in Direct Measures of Job Skill Requirements," 2000; Michael Jeremy Handel, *Measuring Job Content: Skills, Technology, and Management Practices* (Madison: University of Wisconsin, Institute for Research on Poverty, 2008); Chris Warhurst, Chris Tilly, and Mary Gatta, *A New Social Construction of Skill* (Oxford: Oxford University Press, 2017); John Buchanan, David

Finegold, Ken Mayhew, and Chris Warhurst, "Skills and Training: Multiple Targets, Shifting Terrain," in *The Oxford Handbook of Skills and Training*, ed. Chris Warhurst, Ken Mayhew, David Finegold, and John Buchanan (Oxford: Oxford University Press, 2017).

48. Weaver and Osterman, "Skill Demands and Mismatch in US Manufacturing"; D. W. Livingstone, "Skill Underutilization," in *The Oxford Handbook of Skills and Training*, ed. Chris Warhurst, Ken Mayhew, David Finegold, and John Buchanan (Oxford: Oxford University Press, 2017), 322–344; Andrew Weaver, "Beyond Years of Schooling: Precisely Measured Skills, Skill Formation and Economic Growth," in *A Research Agenda for Regeneration Economies*, ed. John Bryson, Lauren Andres, and Rachel Mulhall, Reading City-Regions (Cheltenham: Elgar Research Agendas, 2018).

49. Jörgen Sandberg, "Understanding Human Competence at Work: An Interpretative Approach," *Academy of Management Journal* 43, no. 1 (2000): 9–25.

50. Michael Jeremy Handel, *Worker Skills and Job Requirements: Is There a Mismatch?* (Washington, DC: Economic Policy Institute, 2005).

51. Handel, *Worker Skills and Job Requirements*; Fran Stewart, *The STEM Dilemma: Skills That Matter to Regions* (Kalamazoo, MI: W. E. Upjohn Institute, 2017).

52. Jörgen Sandberg, "How Do We Justify Knowledge Produced within Interpretive Approaches?," *Organizational Research Methods* 8, no. 1 (2005): 41–68; Richard Sennett, *The Craftsman* (New Haven, CT: Yale University Press, 2008).

53. Barbara Rogoff and Jean Lave, eds., *Everyday Cognition: Its Development in Social Context* (Cambridge, MA: Harvard University Press, 1984); Jean Lave and Etienne Wenger, *Situated Learning: Legitimate Peripheral Participation* (Cambridge: Cambridge University Press, 1991).

54. Attewell, "What Is Skill?," 425.

55. Sandberg, "Understanding Human Competence at Work."

56. Natasha Iskander and Nichola Lowe, "Hidden Talent: Tacit Skill Formation and Labor Market Incorporation of Latino Immigrants in the United States," *Journal of Planning Education and Research* 30, no. 2 (September 17, 2010): 132–146; Mike Rose, *The Mind at Work: Valuing the Intelligence of the American Worker* (New York: Penguin, 2005); David W. Livingstone, *Education & Jobs: Exploring the Gaps* (Toronto: University of Toronto Press, 2009); Jonathan Rothwell, "The Hidden STEM Economy" (Washington, DC: Brookings Institution, Metropolitan Policy Program, 2013).

57. Rogoff and Lave, *Everyday Cognition*; Jean Lave, Michael Murtaugh, and Olivia de la Rocha, "The Dialectic of Arithmetic in Grocery Shopping," in *Everyday Cognition: Its Development in Social Context*, ed. Barbara Rogoff and Jean Lave (Cambridge, MA: Harvard University Press, 1984).

58. Wendy L. Millroy, "An Ethnographic Study of the Mathematical Ideas of a Group of Carpenters," *Learning and Individual Differences* 3, no. 1 (1991): 1–25.

59. Houman Harouni, "Toward a Political Economy of Mathematics Education," *Harvard Educational Review* 85, no. 1 (April 2015): 50–74.

60. John Seely Brown and Paul Duguid, "The Social Life of Information," *Harvard Educational Review* 71, no. 1 (2001): 151–152; Jörgen Sandberg, "Competence—the Basis for a Smart Workforce," in *Training for a Smart Workforce*, ed. Rod Gerber and Colin Lankshear (Abingdon: Routledge, 2002), 59–84; Iskander and Lowe, "Immigration and the Politics of Skill"; Matthew Desmond, *On the Fireline: Living and Dying with Wildland Firefighters* (Chicago: University of Chicago Press, 2008).

61. Iskander and Lowe, "Hidden Talent"; Doeringer and Piore, *International Labor Markets and Manpower Analysis*; Attewell, "What Is Skill?"

62. Sandberg, "Understanding Human Competence at Work."

63. Sandberg, "Understanding Human Competence at Work," 21.

64. Natasha Iskander, Nichola Lowe, and Christine Riordan, "The Rise and Fall of a Micro-Learning Region: Mexican Immigrants and Construction in Center-South Philadelphia," *Environment and Planning A* 42, no. 7 (2010): 1595–1612; Nichola Lowe and Natasha Iskander, "Power through Problem Solving: Latino Immigrants and the Inconsistencies of Economic Restructuring," *Population, Space and Place* 23, no. 7 (2017): e2023.

65. Tom Juravich, *Chaos on the Shop Floor: A Worker's View of Quality, Productivity, and Management* (Philadelphia: Temple University Press, 1988).

66. Iskander and Lowe, "Immigration and the Politics of Skill"; Warhurst, Tilly, and Gatta, *A New Social Construction of Skill*.

67. Joseph S. Nye, "Soft Power," *Foreign Policy* 80 (1990): 153–171; Nicholas Wise and Kelly Maguire, "Places, Practices and (Soft) Power," *Local Economy* 34, no. 7 (2019).

68. Gary S. Becker, *Human Capital: A Theoretical and Empirical Analysis, with Special Reference to Education* (Chicago: University of Chicago Press, 2009).

69. David H. Autor, "Why Do Temporary Help Firms Provide Free General Skills Training?," *Quarterly Journal of Economics* 116, no. 4 (2001): 1409–1448.

70. Daron Acemoglu and Jörn-Steffen Pischke, "Beyond Becker: Training in Imperfect Labour Markets," *Economic Journal* 109, no. 453 (1999): 112–142.

71. Nancy MacLean, *Freedom Is Not Enough: The Opening of the American Workplace* (Cambridge, MA: Harvard University Press, 2008).

72. Palladino, *Skilled Hands, Strong Spirits*; Iskander and Lowe, "Immigration and the Politics of Skill"; Jeffrey W. Riemer and Roy Gustav Francis, *Hard Hats: The Work World of Construction Workers* (Beverly Hills, CA: Sage, 1979); David Weil, "Building Safety: The Role of Construction Unions in the Enforcement of OSHA," *Journal of Labor Research* 13, no. 1 (1992): 121–132; Dale Belman, "Unions, the Quality of

Labor Relations, and Firm Performance," *Unions and Economic Competitiveness*, 1992, 41–107; Steven G. Allen, "Unionized Construction Workers Are More Productive," *Quarterly Journal of Economics* 99, no. 2 (1984): 251–274.

73. Doeringer and Piore, *International Labor Markets and Manpower Analysis*.

74. Anthony P. Carnevale, Leila J. Gainer, and A. S. Meltzer, *Workplace Basics: The Skills Employers Want* (Washington, DC: American Society for Training and Development and US Department of Labor, 1988); Sumner H. Slichter, James J. Healy, and E. Robert Livernash, *The Impact of Collective Bargaining on Management* (Washington, DC: Brookings Institution Press, 1960).

75. Holzer and Lerman, "America's Forgotten Middle-Skill Jobs"; Thomas Kochan, David Finegold, and Paul Osterman, "Who Can Fix the 'Middle-Skills' Gap?," *Harvard Business Review* 90, no. 12 (2012): 81–90.

76. Kathleen Thelen, *How Institutions Evolve: The Political Economy of Skills in Germany, Britain, the United States, and Japan* (Cambridge: Cambridge University Press, 2004); Wolfgang Streeck, "Skills and the Limits of Neo-Liberalism: The Enterprise of the Future as a Place of Learning," *Work, Employment and Society* 3, no. 1 (March 1989): 89–104.

77. Meric S. Gertler, "'Being There': Proximity, Organization, and Culture in the Development and Adoption of Advanced Manufacturing Technologies," *Economic Geography* 71, no. 1 (1995): 1–26.

78. Margaret Weir, *Politics and Jobs: The Boundaries of Employment Policy in the United States* (Princeton, NJ: Princeton University Press, 1993); Thelen, *How Institutions Evolve*.

79. Miriam J. Wells, *Strawberry Fields: Politics, Class, and Work in California Agriculture* (Ithaca, NY: Cornell University Press, 1996); Julian E. Orr, *Talking about Machines: An Ethnography of a Modern Job* (Ithaca, NY: Cornell University Press, 2016).

80. Juravich, *Chaos on the Shop Floor*.

81. Harry Braverman, *Labor and Monopoly Capital: The Degradation of Work in the Twentieth Century* (New York: New York University Press, 1998).

82. Osterman, *Securing Prosperity*; William Lazonick, *Competitive Advantage on the Shop Floor* (Cambridge, MA: Harvard University Press, 1990).

83. Doeringer and Piore, *International Labor Markets and Manpower Analysis*, 20.

84. Michael Burawoy, *Manufacturing Consent: Changes in the Labor Process under Monopoly Capitalism* (Chicago: University of Chicago Press, 1982).

85. Thelen, *How Institutions Evolve*.

86. Batt and Appelbaum, *The New American Workplace*.

87. Paul Osterman, "How Common Is Workplace Transformation and Who Adopts It?," *ILR Review* 47, no. 2 (1994): 173–188.

88. Paul S. Adler and R. E. Cole, "Designed for Learning: A Tale of Two Auto Plants," *MIT Sloan Management Review*, April 15, 1993; Kochan and Rubinstein, "Toward a Stakeholder Theory of the Firm."

89. Harley Shaiken, "Beyond Lean Production," *Stanford Law and Policy Review* 5 (1993): 41.

90. Eileen Appelbaum, Thomas Bailey, Peter Berg, Arne L. Kalleberg, and Thomas Andrew Bailey, *Manufacturing Advantage: Why High-Performance Work Systems Pay Off* (Ithaca, NY: Cornell University Press, 2000); Kochan, Lansbury, and MacDuffie, *After Lean Production*.

91. Osterman, "How Common Is Workplace Transformation and Who Adopts It?"; Osterman, *Securing Prosperity*; Jody Knauss, "Modular Mass Production: High Performance on the Low Road," *Politics & Society* 26, no. 2 (1998): 273–296; Thomas R. Bailey and Annette D. Bernhardt, "In Search of the High Road in a Low-Wage Industry," *Politics & Society* 25, no. 2 (1997): 179–201.

92. Shaiken, "Beyond Lean Production"; Osterman, *Securing Prosperity*.

93. Shaiken, "Beyond Lean Production."

## Chapter 3

1. Tom Morrison et al., "Boiling Point? The Skills Gap in U.S. Manufacturing" (Deloitte Development and Manufacturing Institute, 2011), http://www.themanufacturinginsti tute.org/~/media/A07730B2A798437D98501E798C2E13AA.ashx.

2. Manufacturing Institute, "Median Age of the Manufacturing Workforce," October 2013, http://www.themanufacturinginstitute.org/Research/Facts-About-Manufacturing /Workforce-and-Compensation/Median-Age/Median-Age.aspx.

3. Lawrence Mishel, John Schmitt, and Heidi Shierholz, "Assessing the Job Polarization Explanation of Growing Wage Inequality," EPI Working Paper 295 (Washington, DC: Economic Policy Institute, 2013).

4. Peter Cappelli, *Why Good People Can't Get Jobs: The Skills Gap and What Companies Can Do about It* (Philadelphia: Wharton School Press, 2012); Paul Osterman and Andrew Weaver, "Why Claims of Skills Shortages in Manufacturing Are Overblown," EPI Issue Brief 376 (Washington, DC: Economic Policy Institute, 2014); Paul Osterman and Andrew Weaver, "Skills and Skill Gaps in Manufacturing," in *Production in the Innovation Economy*, ed. Richard M. Locke and Rachel L. Wellhausen (Cambridge, MA: MIT Press, 2014), 17–50.

5. Sarah Webster, "No U.S. Skills Gap? Really?," *Huffington Post*, December 4, 2012.

6. Marc Doussard, "Equity Planning Outside City Hall: Rescaling Advocacy to Confront the Sources of Urban Problems," *Journal of Planning Education and Research* 35, no. 3 (2015): 296–306; Laura Dresser, "Human Capital in Context: Policies That Shape Urban Labor Markets," *Jobs and the Labor Force of Tomorrow: Migration, Training, Education*, ed. Michael Papagano (Urbana: University of Illinois Press, 2018), 25–44.

7. Wolfgang Streeck, "Skills and the Limits of Neo-Liberalism: The Enterprise of the Future as a Place of Learning," *Work, Employment and Society* 3, no. 1 (March 1989): 89–104.

8. Cappelli, *Why Good People Can't Get Jobs*; Zeynep Ton, *The Good Jobs Strategy: How the Smartest Companies Invest in Employees to Lower Costs and Boost Profits* (New York: Houghton Mifflin Harcourt, 2014).

9. Robert Giloth, ed., *Workforce Intermediaries: For the 21st Century* (Philadelphia: Temple University Press, 2010); Greg Schrock, "Reworking Workforce Development: Chicago's Sectoral Workforce Centers," *Economic Development Quarterly* 27, no. 3 (2013): 163–178; Annette Bernhardt, Laura Dresser, and Joel Rogers, "Taking the High Road in Milwaukee: The Wisconsin Regional Training Partnership," *WorkingUSA* 5, no. 3 (2001): 109–130; Annette Bernhardt, Laura Dresser, and Joel Rogers, "The Wisconsin Regional Training Partnership," in *Partnering for Change: Unions and Community Groups Build Coalitions for Economic Justice*, ed. David B. Reynolds (Armonk, NY: M. E. Sharpe, 2004), 231; Maureen Conway, *The Garment Industry Development Corporation: A Case Study of a Sectoral Employment Development Approach*, Sectoral Employment Development Learning Project Case Studies Series (New York: Aspen Institute, 1999); Maureen Conway and Robert P. Giloth, *Connecting People to Work: Workforce Intermediaries and Sector Strategies*, ed. Maureen Conway and Robert P. Giloth (New York: American Assembly and Columbia University, 2014).

10. Richard Kazis, "What Do Workforce Intermediaries Do?," in *Workforce Intermediaries for the Twenty-First Century*, ed. Robert P. Giloth (Philadelphia: Temple University Press, 2004).

11. Cindy Marano and Kim Tarr, "The Workforce Intermediary: Profiling the Field of Practice and Its Challenges," in *Workforce Intermediaries: For the Twenty-First Century*, ed. Robert P. Giloth (Philadelphia: Temple University Press, 2004), 931–123.

12. Giloth, *Workforce Intermediaries*.

13. Brenda Lautsch and Paul Osterman, "Changing the Constraints: A Successful Employment and Training Strategy," in *Jobs and Economic Development: Strategies and Practice*, ed. Robert P. Giloth (Newbury Park, CA: Sage, 1998), 214–233.

14. Conway and Giloth, *Connecting People to Work*.

15. Paul Osterman, "Policies Aimed at the Demand Side of the Low-Wage Labor Market," in *A Future of Good Jobs? America's Challenge in the Global Economy*, ed. Timothy J. Bartik and Susan N. Houseman (Kalamazoo, MI: W. E. Upjohn Institute, 2008), 203.

16. Annette D. Bernhardt, Heather Boushey, Laura Dresser, and Chris Tilly, eds., *The Gloves-off Economy: Workplace Standards at the Bottom of America's Labor Market* (Ithaca, NY: Cornell University Press, 2008); Christian Zlolniski, "Labor Control and Resistance of Mexican Immigrant Janitors in Silicon Valley." *Human Organization* 62, no. 1 (2003): 39.

17. Marianne Bertrand and Sendhil Mullainathan, "Are Emily and Greg More Employable than Lakisha and Jamal? A Field Experiment on Labor Market Discrimination," *American Economic Review* 94, no. 4 (2004): 991–1013.

18. Cappelli, *Why Good People Can't Get Jobs*, 62.

19. Allison Forbes, "A Measure of Interdependence: Skill in the Supply Chain," *Economic Development Quarterly* 32, no. 4 (2018): 326–340.

20. Rhandi Berth, Laura Dresser, and Emanuel Ubert, "Moving Apprenticeship into Manufacturing's Future: Industrial Manufacturing Technician," University of Wisconsin–Madison, COWS (Center on Wisconsin Strategy), February 2017.

21. Kathleen Thelen, *How Institutions Evolve: The Political Economy of Skills in Germany, Britain, the United States, and Japan* (Cambridge: Cambridge University Press, 2004).

22. Berth, Dresser, and Ubert, "Moving Apprenticeship into Manufacturing's Future: Industrial Manufacturing Technician."

23. Schrock, "Reworking Workforce Development."

24. Kazis, "What Do Workforce Intermediaries Do?"

25. Steven Dawson, "Now or Never: Heeding the Call of Labor Market Demand," The Pinkerton Papers: Job Quality Series (New York: Pinkerton Foundation, September 2017), 1.

26. Dawson, "Now or Never," 2.

27. Joan Fitzgerald, "Moving the Workforce Intermediary Agenda Forward," *Economic Development Quarterly* 18, no. 1 (2004): 3–9; Chris Benner, "Labour Flexibility and Regional Development: The Role of Labour Market Intermediaries," *Regional Studies* 37, no. 6–7 (2003): 621–633; Elsie Harper-Anderson, "Measuring the Connection between Workforce Development and Economic Development: Examining the Role of Sectors for Local Outcomes," *Economic Development Quarterly* 22, no. 2 (2008): 119–135; Marc Doussard, *Degraded Work: The Struggle at the Bottom of the Labor Market* (Minneapolis: University of Minnesota Press, 2013); Jennifer Clark and Susan Christopherson, "Integrating Investment and Equity: A Critical Regionalist Agenda for a Progressive Regionalism," *Journal of Planning Education and Research* 28, no. 3 (2009): 341–354; Chris Benner and Manuel Pastor, *Just Growth: Inclusion and Prosperity in America's Metropolitan Regions* (New York: Routledge, 2013).

28. Clifford A. Lipscomb, Jan Youtie, Philip Shapira, Sanjay Arora, and Andy Krause, "Evaluating the Impact of Manufacturing Extension Services on Establishment

Performance," *Economic Development Quarterly* 32, no. 1 (2018): 29–43; Philipp Brandt, Andrew Schrank, and Josh Whitford, "Brokerage and Boots on the Ground: Complements or Substitutes in the Manufacturing Extension Partnerships?," *Economic Development Quarterly* 32, no. 4 (2018): 288–299.

29. Ranita Jain, Nichola Lowe, Greg Schrock, and Maureen Conway, *Genesis at Work: Evaluating the Effects of Manufacturing Extension on Business Success and Job Quality* (Washington, DC: Aspen Institute, 2019).

30. Dawson, "Now or Never," 4.

31. John Buchanan, Pauline Anderson, and Gail Power, "Skill Ecosystems," in *The Oxford Handbook of Skills and Training* (Oxford: Oxford University Press, 2017), 444–465; Thomas Kochan, David Finegold, and Paul Osterman, "Who Can Fix the 'Middle-Skills' Gap?," *Harvard Business Review* 90, no. 12 (2012): 81–90.

32. Bjørn T. Asheim, Ron Boschma, and Philip Cooke, "Constructing Regional Advantage: Platform Policies Based on Related Variety and Differentiated Knowledge Bases," *Regional Studies* 45, no. 7 (2011): 893–904; Andrew Schrank and Josh Whitford, "Industrial Policy in the United States: A Neo-Polanyian Interpretation," *Politics & Society* 37, no. 4 (2009): 521–553; Maryann Feldman and Nichola Lowe, "Evidence-Based Economic Development Policy," *Innovations: Technology, Governance, Globalization* 11, no. 3–4 (2017): 34–49; Jennifer Clark, "Regeneration Economies: A Research Agenda: Governance, Policy and Regional Development," in *A Research Agenda for Regeneration Economies: Reading City-Regions*, ed. John R. Bryson, Lauren Andres, and Rachel Mulhall (Cheltenham: Elgar Research Agendas, 2018), 126.

## Chapter 4

1. Kimberly A. Gilsdorf, Fay Hanleybrown, and Laryea Dashell, "How to Improve the Engagement and Retention of Young Hourly Workers," *Harvard Business Review*, December 6, 2017.

2. Heather Boushey and Sarah Jane Glynn, "There Are Significant Business Costs to Replacing Employees" (Washington, DC: Center for American Progress, 2012).

3. Suzanne Berger, *Making in America: From Innovation to Market: From Innovation to Market* (Cambridge, MA: MIT Press, 2013).

4. For additional details on the Manufacturing Connect program, see Julianne Stern, "Philanthropic Logics, Transformative Outcomes: A Case Study of Manufacturing Connect's Demand-Side Labor Market Strategies in Chicago's Metal Manufacturing Sector" (master's thesis, University of North Carolina, 2015). A shorter, co-authored version of the Manufacturing Connect case was published as a book chapter; see Nichola Lowe, Julianne Stern, John Bryson and Rachel Mulhall, "Working in a New Generation: Youth Job Creation and Employer Engagement in Urban

Manufacturing," in *Investing in America's Workforce: Improving Outcomes for Workers and Employers,* ed. Stuart Andreason, Todd Greene, Heath Prince, and Carl E. Van Horn (Kalamazoo, MI: W. E. Upjohn Institute for Employment Research; Atlanta: Federal Reserve Bank of Atlanta, 2018).

5. Rick Mattoon and Susan Longworth, "Manufacturing Connect: Teaching Advanced Manufacturing Skills to Inner-City Students.," in *Investing in America's Workforce: Improving Outcomes for Workers and Employers,* ed. Stuart Andreason, Todd Greene, Heath Prince, and Carl E. Van Horn al. (Kalamazoo, MI: W. E. Upjohn Institute; Atlanta: Federal Reserve Bank of Atlanta, 2018).

6. Pierre Clavel and Robert Giloth, "Planning for Manufacturing: Chicago after 1983," *Journal of Planning History* 14, no. 1 (2015): 19–37.

7. Joan Fitzgerald and Nancey Green Leigh, *Economic Revitalization: Cases and Strategies for City and Suburb* (Newbury Park, CA: Sage, 2002).

8. See the Chicago Manufacturing Renaissance Council's website at https://www.mfgren.org/cmrc.

9. Dan Swinney, "Austin Polytech: Building the Road as We Travel" (Chicago: Center for Labor and Community Research, 2010).

10. Dan Swinney, "Austin Polytech, Manufacturing Renaissance, and Manufacturing Connect" (Chicago: Center for Labor and Community Research, 2014).

11. Swinney, "Austin Polytech: Building the Road as We Travel," 5.

12. AFL-CIO, *Austin Polytechnical Academy,* video (Chicago, 2014), https://youtu.be/LzhPfFgZum0.

13. This section and the following have been adapted from a published book chapter. While that original chapter was co-authored with Julie Stern, John Bryson, and Rachel Mulhall, Nichola Lowe was the primary author for the original versions of these adapted sections and has received permission from the co-authors and book editors to draw on and modify them.

14. Thomas R. Bailey, *Learning to Work: Employer Involvement in School-to-Work Transition Programs* (Washington, DC: Brookings Institution Press, 2010); Thomas Bailey, Katherine Hughes, and Tavis Barr, "Achieving Scale and Quality in School-to-Work Internships: Findings from Two Employer Surveys," *Educational Evaluation and Policy Analysis* 22, no. 1 (2000): 41–64.

## Chapter 5

1. Community College Consortium for Bioscience Credentials, "Forsyth Tech Delivers 'Invaluable Training' Opportunities to Herbalife Employees," National Center for Biotechnology Workforce, Winston-Salem, NC, 2016, http://www.themanufacturing

institute.org/Skills-Certification/Educator-Resources/Best-Practices/~/media/961ABC11
718B4761B1B872966C45EC90.ashx.

2. Robert P. Giloth, ed., *Workforce Intermediaries: For the 21st Century* (Philadelphia: Temple University Press, 2004).

3. Joan Fitzgerald, *Moving up in the New Economy: Career Ladders for US Workers* (Ithaca, NY: Cornell University Press, 2006).

4. Maryann P. Feldman and Nichola J. Lowe, "Restructuring for Resilience," *Innovations: Technology, Governance, Globalization* 6, no. 1 (2011): 129–146.

5. Nichola Lowe and Maryann Feldman, "Constructing Entrepreneurial Advantage: Consensus Building, Technological Uncertainty and Emerging Industries," *Cambridge Journal of Regions, Economy and Society* 1, no. 2 (2008): 265–284.

6. North Carolina Biotechnology Center, "Report to the Joint Legislative Commission on Governmental Operations and the Fiscal Research Division," 2013.

7. John Balchunas, interview with author, 2019.

8. Nichola Lowe, Harvey Goldstein, and Mary Donegan, "Patchwork Intermediation: Challenges and Opportunities for Regionally Coordinated Workforce Development," *Economic Development Quarterly* 25, no. 2 (2011): 158–171.

9. Lowe, Goldstein, and Donegan, "Patchwork Intermediation."

10. Nichola J. Lowe and Laura Wolf-Powers, "Who Works in a Working Region? Inclusive Innovation in the New Manufacturing Economy," *Regional Studies* 52, no. 6 (2018): 828–39.

11. TEConomy/BIO, "The Value of Bioscience Innovation in Growing Jobs and Improving Quality of Life" (Columbus: TEConomy/BIO, 2016).

12. Battelle Technology Partnership Practice, *Impact of Life Sciences in North Carolina* (Columbus: Battelle Memorial Institute, 2014).

13. Battelle Technology Partnership Practice, *Impact of Life Sciences in North Carolina*.

14. Gary P. Pisano and Willy C. Shih, *Producing Prosperity: Why America Needs a Manufacturing Renaissance* (Boston: Harvard Business Press, 2012).

15. Jennifer Clark, *Working Regions: Reconnecting Innovation and Production in the Knowledge Economy* (New York: Routledge, 2013); Marc Doussard and Greg Schrock. "Uneven Decline: Linking Historical Patterns and Processes of Industrial Restructuring to Future Growth Trajectories," *Cambridge Journal of Regions, Economy and Society* 8, no. 2 (2015): 149–165. Suzanne Berger, *How We Compete: What Companies around the World Are Doing to Make It in Today's Global Economy* (New York: Currency Doubleday, 2006).

16. Lowe and Wolf-Powers, "Who Works in a Working Region?"

17. Battelle Technology Partnership/BIO, *Battelle/BIO State Biosciences Jobs, Investments, and Innovation* (Columbus: Battelle Memorial Institute, 2014).

18. Nichola Lowe and Maryann P. Feldman, "Breaking the Waves: Innovating at the Intersections of Economic Development," *Economic Development Quarterly* 32, no. 3 (2018): 183–194.

19. Robert P. Giloth, ed., *Jobs and Economic Development: Strategies and Pratice* (Thousand Oaks, CA: Sage, 1998); Paul Osterman, "Employment and Training Policies: New Directions for Less-Skilled Adults," in *Reshaping the American Workforce in a Changing Economy*, ed. Harry J. Holzer and Demetra Smith Nightingale (Washington, DC: Urban Institute Press, 2007), 119–54.

20. Hilary Pollan, "Case Study: North Carolina BioNetwork's Expansion to Include Food, Beverage and Natural Products in Their Services to the Life Science Sector," class paper, University of North Carolina–Chapel Hill, April 2017.

## Chapter 6

1. See the website for Factory OS at https://factoryos.com.

2. Neil Patel, "90% of Startups Fail: Here's What You Need To Know about the 10%," *Forbes*, January 16, 2015.

3. Fred Block, "Swimming against the Current: The Rise of a Hidden Developmental State in the United States," *Politics & Society* 36, no. 2 (2008): 169–206; Mariana Mazzucato, *The Entrepreneurial State: Debunking Public vs. Private Sector Myths*, vol. 1 (New York: Anthem Press, 2015); Andrew Schrank and Josh Whitford, "Industrial Policy in the United States: A Neo-Polanyian Interpretation," *Politics & Society* 37, no. 4 (2009): 521–553.

4. Amos Zehavi and Dan Breznitz, "Distribution Sensitive Innovation Policies: Conceptualization and Empirical Examples," *Research Policy* 46, no. 1 (2017): 327–336.

5. Jennifer Clark, "Is There a Progressive Approach to Innovation Policy?," *Progressive Planning Magazine*, 2012, 7.

6. Daniel M. Bernhofen, Zouheir El-Sahli, and Richard Kneller, "Estimating the Effects of the Container Revolution on World Trade," *Journal of International Economics* 98 (2016): 7.

7. Bernhofen, El-Sahli, and Kneller, "Estimating the Effects of the Container Revolution on World Trade."

8. Marc Levinson, *The Box: How the Shipping Container Made the World Smaller and the World Economy Bigger-with a New Chapter by the Author* (Princeton, NJ: Princeton University Press, 2016).

9. Kristen Monaco and Lindy Olsson, "Labor at the Ports: A Comparison of the ILA and ILWU" (Long Beach, CA: METRANS Transportation Center, 2005); Paul T. Hartman, *Collective Bargaining and Productivity: The Longshore Mechanization Agreement* (Berkeley and Los Angeles: University of California Press, 1969); Arthur Donovan, "Longshoremen and Mechanization," *Journal for Maritime Research* 1, no. 1 (1999): 66–75.

10. Emil Bjarnason, "Mechanisation and Collective Bargaining in the British Columbia Longshore Industry" (PhD diss., Simon Fraser University, 1975); Hartman, *Collective Bargaining and Productivity.*

11. Bjarnason, "Mechanisation and Collective Bargaining in the British Columbia Longshore Industry.," v.

12. Steven Greenhouse, *The Big Squeeze: Tough Times for the American Worker* (New York: Anchor Books, 2009).

13. Jackie Goodman, "Union Workers Face the Threat of Customer Service Robots in Las Vegas," *Filthy Lucre*, August 20, 2018, https://filthylucre.com/union-workers -face-the-threat-of-customer-service-robots-in-las-vegas.

14. Lulu Garcia-Navarro, "The Robots Are Coming to Las Vegas," *NPR Weekend Edition Sunday*, October 7, 2019.

15. Serena Maria Daniels, "When We Talk about Automation We Also Need to Talk about Race," *Huffington Post*, June 16, 2018.

16. Richard B. Freeman, "Who Owns the Robots Rules the World," *IZA World of Labor*, 2015.

17. Erin Winick, "Confessions of an Accidental Job Destroyer," *MIT Technology Review*, 2018, 37.

18. Winick, "Confessions of an Accidental Job Destroyer," 37.

19. Ranita Jain, Nichola Lowe, Greg Schrock, and Maureen Conway, *Genesis at Work: Evaluating the Effects of Manufacturing Extension on Business Success and Job Quality* (Washington, DC: Aspen Institute, 2019).

20. Jennifer Clark and Marc Doussard, "Devolution, Disinvestment and Uneven Development: US Industrial Policy and Evolution of the National Network for Manufacturing Innovation," *Cambridge Journal of Regions, Economy and Society* 12, no. 2 (2019): 251–270; Fred Block, Matthew R. Keller, and Marian Negoita, "Network Failure and the Evolution of the US Innovation System," *Journal of Industry, Competition and Trade*, 2020, 1–13.

21. See the website of the Advanced Robotics for Manufacturing Institute at https:// arminstitute.org/portfolio-posts/selected-ewd-projects-fall-2017-project-call.

22. Frank Emspak, "Workers, Unions, and New Technology," in *Participatory Design: Principles and Practices*, ed. Douglas Schuler and Aki Namioka (Boca Raton, FL: CRC Press, 1993), 21.

23. Massachusetts Center of Excellence Corporation, "An Introduction to the Centers of Excellence," 1988, 3, https://archives.lib.state.ma.us/bitstream/handle/2452/49629/ocm31065233.pdf?sequence=1.

24. Jennifer Clark, *Uneven Innovation: The Work of Smart Cities* (New York: Columbia University Press, 2020); Ben Green, *The Smart Enough City: Putting Technology in Its Place to Reclaim Our Urban Future* (Cambridge, MA: MIT Press, 2019); Karen Chapple, *Planning Sustainable Cities and Regions: Towards More Equitable Development* (New York: Routledge, 2014).

25. Joan Fitzgerald, *Greenovation: Urban Leadership on Climate Change* (Oxford: Oxford University Press, 2020).

26. See the website of the Jobs to Move America coalition at https://jobstomoveamerica.org/resources/us-employment-plan-resources-2.

27. Madeline Janis, Roxana Aslan, and Katherine Hoff, "Harnessing Government Spending to Revitalize Good Manufacturing Jobs" (New York: Century Foundation, October 3, 2017).

28. Nichola Lowe and Brian J. Morton, "Developing Standards: The Role of Community Benefits Agreements in Enhancing Job Quality," *Community Development* 39, no. 2 (2008): 23–35; Laura Wolf-Powers, "Community Benefits Agreements and Local Government: A Review of Recent Evidence," *Journal of the American Planning Association* 76, no. 2 (2010): 141–159.

29. Carl Benedikt Frey and Michael A. Osborne, "The Future of Employment: How Susceptible Are Jobs to Computerisation?," Working paper, Oxford Martin School (Oxford: Oxford University, 2013).

30. Carl Benedik Frey, *The Technology Trap Capital, Labor, and Power in the Age of Automation* (Princeton, NJ: Princeton University Press, 2019).

31. I thank Frank Levy for suggesting this connection.

32. Nancey Green Leigh and Benjamin R. Kraft, "Emerging Robotic Regions in the United States: Insights for Regional Economic Evolution," *Regional Studies* 52, no. 6 (2018): 804–815.

# Index